2000

Dear Finn
I met Mary Seeley
at the Republican National
Convention. I told her
all about you. I hope
you enjoy reading her
great book about two
of my favorite things
* U.S. Presidents
and
CHRISTMAS

Love
Gram

Grandmother Remembers,

Christmas at the
White House

Grandmother Remembers, Christmas at the White House

Mary Evans Seeley

Illustrated by Terri Sopp Rae

A PRESIDENTIAL CHRISTMAS
Tampa, Florida

Grandmother Remembers:
Christmas at the White House

By Mary Evans Seeley
Illustrated by Terri Sopp Rae

Copyright @2000 by Mary Evans Seeley
Published by A Presidential Christmas
Tampa, Fla.

Includes bibliographical references

Printed and bound in Hong Kong
First Edition 2000

ISBN 0-965-7684-2-2

Reinforced Library Binding
The paintings were rendered in watercolor, pen and ink and color pencil on watercolor paper.
Book typeset in Emtus Regular

Edited by Virginia Koenke Hunt
Designed by Bob Antler, Antler Designworks
Production Manager, Albert Yokum

This book is dedicated to my grandchildren,
Victoria, Andrew, Elizabeth, Lauren and baby Caitlin

Who gave me a reason for reminiscing about our
great American heritage that I wish to pass on to your generation
and to all future generations

ACKNOWLEGMENTS

A huge round of thanks is due the team who brought this book to life, to my illustrator, Terri Sopp Rae; my editor, Virginia Koenke Hunt; my designer, Bob Antler, and my production manager, Albert J. Yokum. I also wish to acknowledge the contributions of Carole Bowers, Claudia Dunne, Marilyn Mayberry, Rex Scouten, Dolores Seeley, Michele Seeley and Kerran Williams for their editorial suggestions.

My sincere appreciation goes to numerous archivists for their unending help in providing photographs from which the illustrations were created. These diligent professionals serve at the following Presidential libraries: Franklin D. Roosevelt Library; Harry S Truman Library, Dwight D. Eisenhower Library, John F. Kennedy Library, Lyndon B. Johnson Library, Richard M. Nixon Museum and Birthplace, Gerald R. Ford Library, Jimmy Carter Library, Ronald Reagan Library, and the George Bush Library.

Finally, and as always, my deepest gratitude to my husband, Ronald Seeley, and our children for their continued support of my literary endeavors.

Preface
To Parents and Grandparents

Christmas is the biggest holiday on the American calendar, and the White House is the home of the nation's Chief Executive. How the most powerful family in the land celebrates the most popular holiday in the land makes for an important story for young readers and listeners. It's important because Presidents in celebration are far more accessible than Presidents being statesmen.

Who can envision Herbert Hoover leaving a Christmas Eve party to climb to the White House roof and watch as fire fighters battled the flames destroying his office? It would surprise many that the President who brought the nation out of the Great Depression and through World War II was also the biggest Christmas fan who ever lived in the White House. Franklin Roosevelt made Christmas into a three-day festival, highlighted by his traditional Christmas Eve reading of Dickens' "Christmas Carol" to his whole family.

Dwight Eisenhower personally painted the art that was reproduced for the gifts he and Mamie gave for Christmas. Lyndon Johnson's Christmas stocking was decorated with a map of Texas, a picture of his LBJ ranch, likenesses of his horse and his dogs, and other symbols of personal significance to him.

First Ladies play a vital part in the festivities too. Eleanor Roosevelt purchased Christmas gifts all year long and stored them in her special Christmas closet. Mamie Eisenhower created a splashy show with her 26 Christmas trees spread throughout the White House. Pat Nixon initiated the Christmastime candlelight tours of the public rooms. Barbara Bush rode a cherry picker to the top of the National Christmas Tree to place the star a record-breaking 12 times; invariably she took along one or two of her grandchildren.

This book is an easy introduction to our Presidents beginning with Calvin Coolidge. It presents them as real people with their own traditions within their own historical milieu. Despite personal differences, however, First Families celebrate Christmas just as do families all across the land. They go Christmas shopping, sing Christmas carols, decorate their own trees and hang stockings. They give Christmas parties and enjoy holiday food. They send Christmas cards and give gifts and wish everyone they talk to or meet a "Merry Christmas."

Please join me and my grandchildren as we visit the White House at this most special time of year.

Mary Evans Seeley

Tori, Andrew and Elizabeth were on vacation with their grandmother in Washington, D.C. "The White House is located here in our nation's capital at 1600 Pennsylvania Avenue," said Grandmother. The White House is a big, beautiful brick and stone house with a big lawn and two fountains. And it is over 200 years old!

"The White House belongs to the American people," said Grandmother, "and we are going inside for a visit."

"Who lives in the White House?" asked Elizabeth.

"The President of the United States lives in the White House with his wife and children," said Grandmother. "We call them the First Family." The family quarters are on the second floor of the house.

"The White House was just being built when George Washington was President," said Grandmother. Our second President, John Adams, was the first person to live in it. He moved in on November 1, 1800. The next day he wrote a prayer that every President who lived in the house would be wise and honest. The President's words were carved into the mantel over the fireplace in the State Dining Room.

There are 132 rooms in the White House. The public may visit only a few of them. "Which rooms are we going to see?" asked Elizabeth.

"Public tours of the main floor begin in the East Room," said Grandmother. "That's the largest room in the house. It is used for big parties, concerts and press conferences." Paintings of George and Martha Washington hang on the East Room walls.

The State Dining Room is where important dinners are held. One hundred and forty guests can eat there at the same time. This is where you can read John Adams' prayer on the mantel. Above the mantel hangs a painting of Abraham Lincoln.

The White House is like a museum. The Red Room, Blue Room and Green Room are filled with many beautiful paintings and old furniture. These rooms are used for tea parties and small receptions. The Blue Room is where the decorated indoor tree stands every Christmas. Right over the Blue Room is the Yellow Oval Room used only by the First Family. It has a balcony named for President Harry Truman. From the Truman Balcony the First Family can look out over the South Lawn of the White House and see the Washington Monument.

"Does the President celebrate Christmas in the White House?" asked Andrew.

"Oh, yes," said Grandmother, "The First Family celebrates Christmas much like we do. Many workers help them get ready. Christmas trees are decorated throughout the whole house. Wreaths, flowers and festive garlands turn the house into a holiday wonderland. Some say it is magical."

12

The First Family invites their friends
and important leaders to visit. They all
enjoy the decorations, eat the holiday
food and listen to music of the season.
The First Family gives hundreds of gifts.
They send thousands of Christmas cards
to people both near and far. The
President and his wife, the First Lady,
even sing Christmas carols.

13

One special job of the President is to light the National Christmas Tree that grows near the White House. In the early years, the President lit the tree's lights on Christmas Eve. Bands played, choirs sang and everyone joined in.

This all began during the early days of radio. People all across America turned on their brand-new radios and listened to Christmas carols. They liked to hear news from Washington. They especially wanted to hear the voice of the President greeting them at Christmas.

Today the celebration is called the Pageant of Peace. The President still makes a holiday speech and lights the National Christmas Tree. People who live in Washington still enjoy the ceremony. One change is that now the ceremony is held early in December instead of on Christmas Eve. Another change is that now all Americans can see the festivities on television. There is more music and speaking, and even Santa pays a fun-filled visit.

"Who started the tradition of lighting the National Christmas tree?" asked Tori.
"Calvin Coolidge was the first President to light the National Christmas Tree,"
said Grandmother. "It was way back in 1923, when my mother was a little girl."
President Coolidge was a such a quiet man that he was known as "Silent Cal." No
one was really surprised that he never said a word at the ceremony. Four more
Christmas Eve ceremonies came and went. He still did not speak to the people.
Finally, on his last Christmas in the White House, he spoke his holiday best wishes
to the American people before he lit the tree.

"How did his family celebrate Christmas?" asked Tori.

"The President's wife, Grace, did something very special," said Grandmother. "She invited everyone to the White House lawn on Christmas Eve for holiday music." The First Lady had her church choir sing carols on the steps of the White House. *The Evening Star* newspaper printed the words to the songs. Ten thousand people who wanted to sing or listen came to the White House with their words from the paper and a light of their own. Thousands more all across the country enjoyed the Christmas music with the First Family by listening on the radio.

Our next President was Herbert Hoover. He and his wife, who was called Lou Henry, had grandchildren. The Hoovers took them along when the President went to light the National Christmas Tree. The President wished every home in America a Merry Christmas and a Happy New Year over the radio. Then the First Family went back to the White House for a dinner party. One Christmas Eve, as the President and his guests ate dessert, someone whispered to him that the White House was on fire! He walked quickly to the fire. His very own office was in flames! The President climbed to the roof and watched the fire fighters from there.

"What did the people at the party do?" asked Andrew.

"The dinner party went on," said Grandmother. Mrs. Hoover had heard about the fire, but stayed very calm. The Marine band played as loud as it could. They did not want anyone to hear the fire engines outside. Then there were gifts for all. When the party ended, Mrs. Hoover took her guests to a safe place outside and they all watched. Much of the President's office was burned, but many of his papers were saved. The next Christmas, a red toy fire truck was one of the gifts the President gave.

"That's cool," said Andrew.

"Do any of you know," asked Grandmother, "who was President longest of all?"

Said Tori, "Wasn't it Franklin Delano Roosevelt, who was the President during World War II?"

"You're right," said Grandmother. "They called him by his initials, FDR, and he was in the White House for 12 whole years." And 12 Christmases, too."

The Roosevelts loved everything about Christmas. The President's wife, Eleanor, shopped all year for hundreds of Christmas gifts for their staff and the children of their staff. All year she hid her gifts in her special Christmas closet. Just before Christmas, the President's children, grandchildren and mother all came to spend several days at the White House.

On Christmas Eve, the First Family decorated their tree. While the family did the work, the President told them where to hang each ornament.

The favorite part of the evening was when the President read the "Christmas Carol" by Charles Dickens. He used a different voice for Scrooge and Fezziwig and all the ghosts. As much as the children loved the way the story came alive, no one enjoyed the reading more than did the President himself. Then the Roosevelts, old and young alike, marched up to FDR's bedroom to hang their stockings on his fireplace mantel. On Christmas morning, the children awakened their grandfather by jumping onto his bed. Even the President of the United States got up early for a Roosevelt family Christmas.

FDR celebrated Christmas in the White House for the first 10 years he was President. By 1943, American soldiers had been fighting World War II for more than two years. Because of the war, the National Christmas Tree in Washington did not have lights. The President, tired from the stress of being Commander-in-Chief, went to his home in Hyde Park, New York, for Christmas. Everyone could hear his Christmas Eve message from Hyde Park on the radio.

The war was almost over in 1945, when Harry Truman became
President. It was hard work to make peace, bring all the soldiers home and
get them jobs. The President drew great strength from going back to his
home in Independence, Missouri. For his first two Christmases as President,
he lit the National Christmas Tree in Washington and then flew home.

"The 1946 ceremony was special," said Grandmother. "For the very
first time, television cameras were there, and many Americans could see
everything as it was taking place."

"Did you watch?" asked Elizabeth.

"No," said Grandmother. "When I was your age, people were just
starting to buy television sets. We didn't have one yet."

In 1948, President Truman became the first President to light the
National Christmas Tree by long distance. Sitting in his living room in
Independence, he made his Christmas speech. Then he turned on a switch
connected with the tree in Washington and all the lights went on.

His last year in office, President Truman and First Lady Bess Truman
celebrated Christmas at the White House. One of their gifts to their staff
was a photograph of the White House. It showed the Truman Balcony,
which the President had added so he and other First Families could enjoy
the view of the South Lawn.

Dwight Eisenhower was a World War II general. He and his wife, Mamie, moved around a lot to wherever the general was stationed. When the Eisenhowers got ready for Christmas in the White House, Mrs. Eisenhower wanted every room decorated. Her staff decorated a total of 26 Christmas trees. There was a tall one in the East Room with silver and white lights. There were little ones on tables and on each side of the fireplace mantel. There were even trees in the laundry room and the maid's sitting room.

One Christmas, the President's son, John, brought word of an extra-special gift. It was a new granddaughter.

"I was born on Christmas Day," piped up Elizabeth.

"Yes," said Grandmother. "I know how happy the First Family must have been to have a new grandchild born at Christmas. You were a very special Christmas gift to our family."

President Eisenhower liked to paint for a hobby.

"What did he paint?" asked Tori.

"He painted pictures of Abraham Lincoln and George Washington," said Grandmother. He also painted pictures of a red barn, a church, a creek where he liked to fish and a mountain that was named after him. The president of the Hallmark Cards Company printed copies of President Eisenhower's paintings. He and Mrs. Eisenhower gave them away as Christmas gifts.

President John Kennedy's children, Caroline and baby John, had many pets. Caroline's pet ducks swam in the fountain on the White House lawn. Her pet terrier, Charlie, ate some of her ducks, so the ducks had to move to Rock Creek Park. Caroline also had a pony named Macaroni. One snowy day in Washington, the children's mother, Jacqueline Kennedy, asked that the sleigh and Macaroni be brought to the South Lawn. She wanted to take Caroline and her playmates for a sleigh ride across the fresh snow.

"Where did Macaroni live?" asked Tori.

Said Grandmother, "There was a stable on the White House grounds."

When they were finished, Mrs. Kennedy unhitched Macaroni from the sleigh and took little John John for a pony ride. Then she led the pony up to the Oval Office for a visit with the President.

A photograph of that day's sleigh ride over the snow was made into a Christmas card. President and Mrs. Kennedy sent 2,000 of them to family and friends, government officials and heads of countries around the world. A photo of Caroline's ducks swimming in the White House fountain became the family's Christmas gift their first year in the White House.

One December, President and Mrs. Lyndon Johnson had a very special family event.

"Did they have a Christmas party?" asked Andrew.

"In a way they did," said Grandmother. "Their daughter, Lynda Bird, was married in the White House early in December." Florists turned the White House into a wedding wonderland with wedding white and Christmas reds and greens. In the East Room, on that big day in 1967, the President and his wife, Lady Bird, gave their daughter in marriage to Marine Captain Charles Robb. The couple cut the first piece from their five-foot cake with the captain's sword. He was soon to be in Vietnam, where American troops were again at war.

The Johnsons had a family tradition of hanging decorated stockings on the fireplace at Christmas. Each person had a special stocking of his or her own. The President's included the Presidential flag; the National Christmas Tree; a shape of the state of Texas; a picture of his LBJ ranch in Texas; his horse, Old Blue; his plane, *Air Force One*; and his dogs, Him and Yuki.

"Those are funny names for dogs," said Andrew.

29

Pat Nixon was a First Lady who liked to plan surprises. At Christmas, she wanted as many people as possible to enjoy the beauty of the White House. Her first surprise was holding candlelight tours of the White House for people who worked during the day. But what about the millions of Americans who could not come to Washington? She surprised them by inviting everyone in the country to visit by television. Viewers enjoyed the White House all decorated for the holidays. They also saw and heard the President, Richard Nixon, and the rest of the family sharing their Christmas thoughts and memories.

"One surprise was three feet tall and weighed 45 pounds," said Grandmother. "It was especially for all the children who came to the White House." Mrs. Nixon asked the White House chef to create a giant gingerbread house for the State Dining Room. It was not finished until Hansel and Gretel were part of the decoration. Now, at every Christmas, a White House chef makes a new gingerbread house for the First Family.

"I like to decorate gingerbread houses," said Elizabeth. "I wish I could have helped."

In 1976 the nation celebrated its 200th birthday. It was a perfect time for Gerald Ford to be President and for Betty Ford to be First Lady. They loved old-fashioned Christmas decorations. For Christmas of 1976, the 20-foot tree in the Blue Room was decorated with 2,500 handmade flowers from people all across the country. The decorations were crafted of silk, felt, beads, shells, ribbon, seeds, bamboo, corn husks, metal, porcelain, and glass. Under the tree were gifts sent by Americans everywhere to remember the nation's special birthday.

"What did the Fords do for fun?" asked Tori.
"Did you ever go to a party with Big Bird?"
said Grandmother.

One Christmas Betty Ford and her
daughter Susan invited the children of foreign
diplomats to the White House for a holiday
party. Many came dressed in the clothes they
wore in their homelands. Big Bird from
Sesame Street put on a show that was fun for
everyone. Even President Ford came by to see
what the excitement was all about.

33

President Jimmy Carter came from the Southern state of Georgia. In 1980, his last Christmas in the White House, he and the First Lady wanted to thank the many people who had worked for them while the President was in office. Treating everyone with Southern hospitality, the Carters threw a giant winter party on the South Lawn. They served hot dogs and popcorn to eat, hot chocolate and apple cider to drink. Unfortunately, the South Lawn that day was just like the South for much of winter. There was no snow, so trucks had to deliver snow for a snowman-making contest. And the judge of the contest was none other than the President of the United States.

There was no ice on the South Lawn either, so carpenters built a skating rink and flooded it with water. After it was frozen, Olympic skater Peggy Fleming and her group entertained the guests. Carolers from nearby churches and schools provided holiday music. The winter party itself was special, but the ending was spectacular. Fireworks formed a huge Christmas card in the sky. They spelled out the words "Merry Christmas." Other fireworks spelled out the names of the President and First Lady. They said, "Jimmy and Rosalynn."

"I wish I lived in the North so I could skate and make a snowman," said Andrew.

Grandmother said, "President Ronald Reagan had a favorite story that he often shared at Christmas."

"Oh, tell us about it," said Tori.

"It was called 'One Solitary Life,'" said Grandmother. President Reagan liked it because it was about the real meaning of Christmas. That's why he always told it the same way to everyone. It did not matter if he was speaking at the lighting of the National Christmas Tree. It did not matter if he was talking to the American people on television or reading to a group of children in the White House. Even Mrs. Reagan and her dog, Rex, enjoyed listening to the story.

The story was about a man named Jesus, whose birth we celebrate at Christmas. The President said that this man never wrote a book. This man never was elected to an office. He never owned a home. He never went to college. He never visited a big city. He never did any of the things a man does to become great. Even 2,000 years after his birth, Jesus is still at the center of Christmas, the President said. The strength of all the world's armies and the power of all the world's rulers put together have not done as much for men and women and boys and girls as this One Solitary Life.

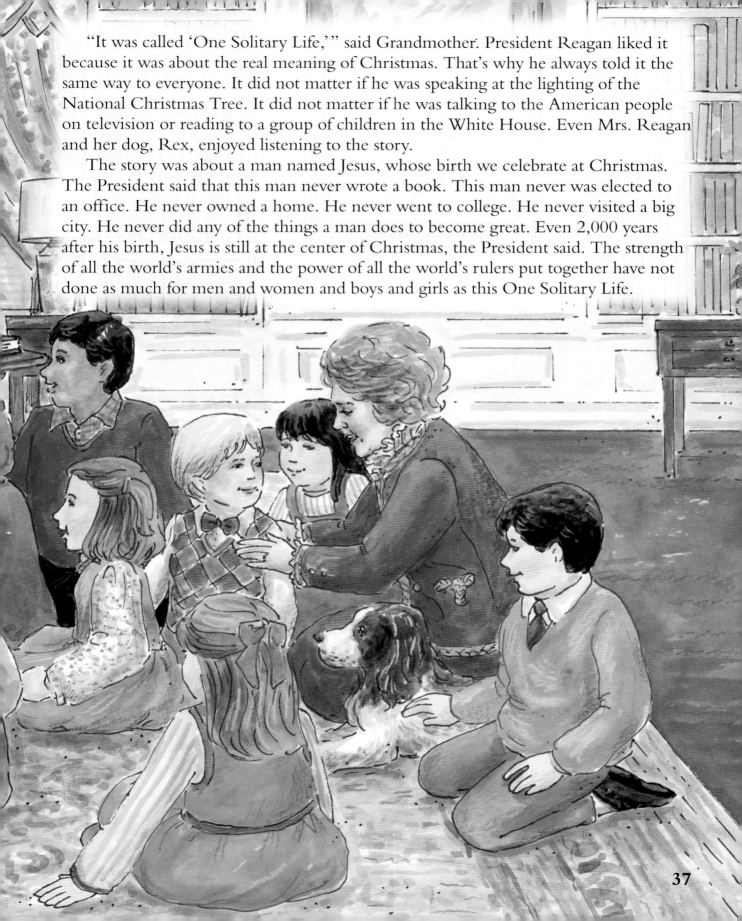

"I'll bet no one knows how the star gets on top of the National Christmas Tree," said Grandmother. While Reagan was President, his wife, Nancy, asked the Vice President's wife, Barbara Bush, to place the star on the tree. After the tree was decorated, Mrs. Bush climbed into a truck's cherry picker and rode all the way to the top. She had such fun that in time she asked some of her grandchildren to ride up with her. When her husband, George Bush, became President, she continued to do this special job every year at Christmas. All in all, Mrs. Bush set the star in place a total of 12 times. She now holds the tree-topping record.

"Wow, Grandmother, would you take me up in a cherry picker?" asked Andrew.

George and Barbara Bush loved to spend Christmas with their five children and 11 grandchildren. The Yellow Oval Room in the family quarters of the White House was decorated with a huge tree. The tree was covered with family ornaments. A manger scene done in needlepoint decorated the table. On the fireplace mantel hung the grandchildren's Christmas stockings. Christmas morning was a time of great joy for all.

The President and First Lady had an artist paint a picture of what the Yellow Oval Room would have looked like on Christmas morning after the grandchildren had opened all their presents. George and Barbara Bush used the painting on their Christmas card in 1991.

The President of the United States is often too busy to go shopping. When he does go to the mall, he is never alone. First, there are all the members of the Secret Service to protect him. Next, there are all the other shoppers who stop what they are doing to watch the President. Bill Clinton liked to go shopping on Christmas Eve. He looked forward to seeing the stores decorated for Christmas and hearing all the holiday music. Because he never got out to shop except at Christmas, the President had a great time looking at all the gift items in their different shapes and colors.

"I wouldn't want everybody looking at us when we go shopping," said Elizabeth.

"Well, that's what it's like to be President," said Grandmother.

The President's daughter, Chelsea, liked to go shopping with her father. Sometimes the First Lady, Hillary, joined them. Despite the commotion it caused at the mall, the Clintons all agreed that getting out for holiday shopping was a lot of fun.

41

The President is the leader of all the people in the country. That is a big job. The President is also called on to solve many problems around the rest of the world. Christmas is the one time every year when he can give gifts, send cards, enjoy the holiday with his family, and decorate a Christmas tree. It is the one time he can enjoy the same holiday traditions that have meant so much to so many Americans for so long.

"Did you enjoy learning about how our First Families celebrate Christmas in the White House?" Grandmother asked.

"Yes, yes," said the children. "Can we come back to visit the White House again next Christmas?"

Historical Notes

To Parents, Grandparents and Teachers

During America's early days, the country's first President, **George Washington**, lived in three houses. Two were in New York and one was in Philadelphia. Neither city was right to serve as the capital. In time, he selected a large tract of land on the Potomac River. The tract was called the District of Columbia, and the capital city within was named for George Washington. Congress purchased the land and the President hired architects to plan the capital's streets, parks and principal buildings of government. Work did not begin until the city plan was finalized. James Hoban designed the President's House, and its cornerstone was laid October 13, 1792.

When the country's second President, **John Adams**, moved into the President's House on November 1, 1800, its exterior was complete, but the inside was not. Much of the flooring remained unfinished and the grand staircase was nothing more than a gaping hole. Nonetheless, on Christmas Day President Adams and his wife, **Abigail**, hosted a reception for members of Congress. In an attempt to dry out the plaster on the walls, 20 cords of wood were burned in the 39 fireplaces. Unfortunately, the executive mansion was still cold and damp when the guests arrived. To add to the First Lady's distress, the guests, unable to find comfort, left early. Even the Adamses' children's party ended in embarrassment. When a playmate broke four-year-old granddaughter Susanna's new set of doll dishes, Susanna bit off the nose and cheeks of the playmate's wax doll. President Adams himself had to make peace between the tiny tots.

The convening of Congress on the first Monday of December traditionally marked the beginning of the holiday season in Washington. For the first hundred years, celebrating Christmas at the White House was kept low-key. Christmas Day was generally spent with family and friends, and worship was a personal matter. By contrast, on New Year's Day of 1801, President **John Adams** began the custom of hosting a formal reception for dignitaries as well as the general public. In 1930, a total of 6,300 people lined up outside the White House to get in. After President **Herbert Hoover** and his wife, **Lou Henry**, shook hands for hours on end, it was decided that the custom should be discontinued. The country's ninth President, **Benjamin Harrison**, introduced a tradition he hoped would be followed by every family in America: He set up the first Christmas tree in the White House.

In 1923 the acting general director of the Community Center Department of the Public Schools of D.C. suggested erecting a Christmas tree on the South Lawn of the White House. The idea was to stage a Christmas Eve celebration in which everyone in the nation's capital might participate. That December a 60-foot tree from President **Calvin Coolidge's** home state of Vermont was set up on the Ellipse. After a number of early attempts to use live trees resulted in great damage to them, the National Christmas Tree Growers Association began providing the National Christmas Tree. In 1978 a live, 32-foot Colorado blue spruce, from York, Pennsylvania, was planted on the Ellipse and is used to this day.

During World War II the Board of Commissioners of the District of Columbia recommended that the National Christmas Tree be abandoned in an effort to conserve electricity as well as the fuel and power to transport people to the White House. With the President away, First Lady **Eleanor Roosevelt** appealed to the board to save the 20-year-old tradition unless abolishing the custom was absolutely necessary. Conforming to government war restrictions, electric lights were not put on the tree. Instead, schoolchildren made ornaments bearing the name of a loved one who was serving in the armed forces.

On December 17, 1954, the Christmas Pageant of Peace was organized to emphasize the desire for peace through the spirit and meaning of Christmas. Over the years, the festival has expanded to include the ceremony at the lighting of the National Christmas Tree, Protestant services, Catholic masses, performances by foreign embassies, a Nativity scene, the Menorah, and state trees decorating the Pathway of Peace.

While Christmas is for children, the President and First Lady have added their own special touch to the holidays. **Calvin Coolidge's** first Christmas message was written out and appeared in newspapers on Christmas morning 1927. **Herbert Hoover** led a procession of children and adults on a Christmas Eve march upstairs and downstairs and all through the White House in search of Santa Claus. **Franklin Roosevelt** invited **Winston Churchill** to speak at the tree lighting ceremony in 1941 as they were together to discuss war strategy. Two years later, FDR decided that he wanted to send the Prime Minister in England a Christmas tree to arrive before Christmas — even if it had to be delivered by a bomber. **Harry Truman** spoke often of the true meaning of Christmas found in the message of the Child of Bethlehem. He said, "We need Christmas to bring us back to a due sense of spiritual values." **Dwight Eisenhower** expanded the role of Presidential Christmas cards and gifts, having painted the art for six of his eight gifts himself. The Eisenhowers sent 38 different cards in the President's years in office, including one in which he and **Mamie** were dressed in Santa Claus suits.

Jacqueline Kennedy delighted the little children with themed Christmas trees; one was decorated with ornaments from Tchaikovsky's *Nutcracker* ballet. **Lady Bird**

Johnson secured for the enjoyment of White House visitors a 30-piece antique crèche, valued at $25,000, which has been on display in the East Room every December since 1967. **Richard Nixon** chose formal portraits of former Presidents to embellish his Christmas gifts to the White House staff. **Betty Ford** offered a White House pamphlet of instructions for families across America on how to make their Christmas ornaments out of scraps of material; in the process, they would also be spending more time together.

Jimmy Carter, to signify the plight of the hostages during the Iranian crisis, decided that the lights on the National Christmas Tree would remain off until the return of the 50 American hostages. In response to seven-year-old Amy Benham's Make a Wish request to help the President turn on the lights of the National Christmas Tree, **Ronald Reagan** invited her to join him on the South Portico and fulfill her dream. **George Bush** offered young visitors to the Oval Office gingerbread cookies that decorated the tree set up in his office. **Bill Clinton** has enjoyed a holiday reading of Clement Moore's "The Night Before Christmas" ever since daughter Chelsea has been a baby.

More historical insight can be found in the author's book, *Season's Greetings From the White House*. Also visit the U.S. government website www.whitehouse.gov and www.whitehousechristmas.com, a website based on the book by Mary Seeley.

BIBLIOGRAPHY

Buckland, Gail. *The White House in Miniature*. New York: W.W. Norton and Company, 1994.

Menendez, Albert. *Christmas in the White House*. Philadelphia: The Westminster Press, 1983.

Rosenbaum, Alvin. *A White House Christmas*. Washington, D.C.: The Preservation Press, 1992.

Seeley, Mary Evans. *Season's Greetings From the White House*. Tampa, Fla.: A Presidential Christmas, 1998.

Walters, Kate. *The Story of the White House*. New York: Scholastic Inc., 1991.

The White House: An Historic Guide. Washington, D.C.: White House Historical Association, 1962.

Also, visit our website at www.whitehousechristmas.com.

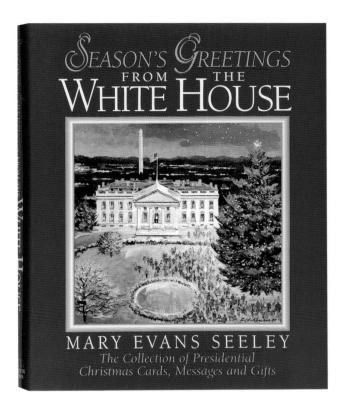

This is the book on which *Grandmother Remembers: Christmas at the White House* is based. Now in its third printing, and written with the cooperation and support of White House curator Rex Scouten, this is the definitive work on the subject. Dating back to the Coolidge administration, Mary Evans Seeley's *Season's Greetings From the White House* tells the full stories of the Presidents' Christmas gifts and cards; hardbound, 224 pages; 8¾ x 11⅛"; 134 photographs, 105 in full color. Visit the website www.whitehousechristmas.com for a comprehensive preview of the book's contents.

You may purchase both of Mary Evans Seeley's books at your local bookstore or gift shop, or you may order directly from the publisher at one of the addresses below.

For ordering and other information,
Website: www.whitehousechristmas.com
E-mail: maryseeley@whitehousechristmas.com

Publisher address:
A Presidential Christmas
P.O. Box 272667
Tampa, FL 33688

For special autographed copies, call 1-800-738-7838.

883
Les

Lessing, Erich

The adventures
of Ulysses

4277

DATE		
JUN 4 1972	MAR 2 2 1993	
AUG 1 8 72		
OCT 1 0 72		
NOV 9 1988		
DEC 1 3 1988		
JAN 17 1989		
OCT 29 1989		
APR 7 1990		
AUG. 1 5 1990		

MENDHAM TOWNSHIP LIBRARY

© THE BAKER & TAYLOR CO.

THE ADVENTURES OF ULYSSES

THE ADVENTURES OF ULYSSES

HOMER'S EPIC IN PICTURES
BY ERICH LESSING

WITH AN INTRODUCTION
"HOMER AND HIS ODYSSEY"
BY KARL KERÉNYI

DODD, MEAD & COMPANY · NEW YORK

The introduction by Karl Kerényi
was adapted by Wolf Stadler and
translated from the original German
by Kevin Smyth, Paris.
Index of plates and bibliography by Cornelia Kerényi.

The text from the Odyssey of Homer,
translated by T. E. Shaw. Copyright 1932
by Bruce Rogert, renewed 1960 by A. W. Lawrence.
Reprinted by permission of
Oxford University Press, Inc., New York.

Published in the United States of America
by Dodd, Mead & Company, 1970.

Original edition: "Die Abenteuer des Odysseus,"
Herder, Freiburg, 1969
First published in West Germany
© 1970 by Herder KG
Printed in West Germany by Herder 1970
Library of Congress Catalog Card Number: 71 – 128865

TRACING THE JOURNEYS OF ULYSSES –
THE STORY OF THIS BOOK

This book tells of the wanderings of Ulysses, the subject of the famous epic of the Greek poet Homer. It is the story of a man who lived more than 3000 years ago, according to tradition. It is full of fantastic adventures, but the real interest of Ulysses is that he became a symbol of human endurance and of man's inventive powers. And behind the story of Ulysses' relentless struggle to reach his homeland is the desire of every man for his home.

This is the timeless element in the figure of Ulysses that has made his story so significant from those far-away times down to the present day. Since the travels of Ulysses, the word "Odyssey" (from another Greek form of the name Odysseus) has been used for dangerous journeys to uncertain goals, such as millions of men had to undertake in the last two World Wars.

How are we to picture this immortal hero? How are we to envisage the places he visited on his travels through the Mediterranean? This book tries to give an answer. It is a picturebook, but in a new style. It does not confine itself to listing the many works of art created by Greek and Roman antiquity apropos of the journeys of Ulysses. And its ultimate effort is not the rediscovery and photographing of Ulysses' landing places, though they are often described in precise detail by Homer. Both forms of presenting the *Odyssey* in pictures have been attempted, but mostly separately, either from the point of view of history of art or from that of geography. Neither approach taken alone seems to give the degree of life and vividness to the immortal figure of Ulysses at which this book has aimed.

André Malraux coined the term, "the museum of the imagination." Such a museum of the imagination exists nowhere – unfortunately, one may say. For the museum of the imagination brings together works of art which are in reality scattered throughout the museums of the world. When Goethe traveled to Italy in 1786, he did what the museum of the imagination would like to offer. He saw only one epoch, the Italy of antiquity. He passed by the glories of the Renaissance, of Baroque and Romanesque art, and the Byzantine mosaics. He traveled to Italy to admire the works of antiquity and he had eyes for nothing else. But what he looked at, he saw well and fixed indelibly in his mind's eye. This is more or less at what the museum of the imagination aims. It tries to give a clear picture of an epoch, and one which will stay. Anyone who has been to Greece, Italy, Spain, or France will remember how many images crowded in on him. And he admits that he often grew tired of all the sightseeing and really lost interest. He went on simply because the visits were on his program and he had paid for his tour. He had an overdose of sights worth seeing. This is the sort of satiety which the museum of the imagination spares us. It is, as this book tries to be, a museum without a director, supervisors, or "do not touch" notices. Here the tourist can stop and gaze as long as he likes, with no guide to move him on.

The aim of this book was to use landscapes and still life in combination with texts from Homer to conjure up a vivid picture of life in the times of Ulysses. It was not an easy task. Erich Lessing traveled some 15,000 miles, in car, train, ship, and airplane, to gather the material for the plates. His efforts to trace Ulysses throughout the museums of the world were also a journey into the unknown. Sometimes days of search were needed to find in fact some representation of Ulysses which was catalogued among the possessions of a museum. The relief showing the ship of Ulysses and the Sirens (Plate 48) was finally discovered, thanks to the tireless efforts of a supervisor, at the top of a twelve-foot-high chest in the cellar of the Louvre. There was another troublesome search for a bronze statuette of Ulysses, only one and a half inches high in the Archaeological Museum of Vienna, the only indication of its location being a reference in the catalogue of the Louvre. The Vienna Museum contains some 4000 small antique bronzes, still not catalogued, but the officials were able to produce the article in the end. We take this opportunity of thanking them, and also all the curators, supervisors, and specialists without whose help the museum of the imagination presented in this book could not have been brought together.

The search for all the places Ulysses visited in the Mediterranean, according to Homer's epic or the researches of scholars, was as taxing as the search of the museums. Erich Lessing himself traveled the routes of Ulysses, as Heinrich Schliemann many years before him had done when this pioneer of Homeric exploration discovered ancient Troy and excavated the citadel of King Atreus at Mycenae. Lessing too followed the text of Homer first and foremost, but used more modern aids. These were the books of the French scholar Victor Bérard, who had taken a photographer with him in 1912 when following the trail of Ulysses, and also the *Ulysses Found* of the English sailor Ernle Bradford, in which Ulysses' wanderings were observed and reconstructed from the point of view of navigation. And Lessing had the same experience as Schliemann, Bérard, Bradford, and many other investigators. Very often, the descriptions in Homer were so exact when read correctly that the places could still be identified unmistakably. Places like the channel between Scylla and Charybdis – the Straits of Messina (Plates 50, 55) – or the island of Djerba, the land of the Lotus-eaters (Plate 33), are described so clearly by Homer, with further navigational indications about distances logged each day and directions of winds, that it would seem that the poet used an ancient manual of sailing ships as the basis of his descriptions.

HOMER AND HIS ODYSSEY

There are other places in the *Odyssey* which cannot be fixed with certainty. This is only to be expected, since Homer constantly combines precise local knowledge and navigational bearings with elements from mythology and legend. His poem is more than the description of adventurous travels. The present book does not try, for instance, to picture the island of Calypso, which some scholars have identified with Malta and others have thought is Atlantis, beyond the Straits of Gibraltar. Homer himself seems to have indicated that this is a mythical place, the "edge of beyond," when he called it the "Navel of the Sea." Navel means the center, but it also means here the point at which the higher regions meet the lower. And Homer also considers this navel as a point which lies on the edge of the world – in keeping with the ancient notion of the world as a floating disc. When Ulysses enters the cave of Calypso, he has reached the "edge." He is on the brink of immortality, since the nymph could have made Ulysses immortal. Can it be that he is also at the brink of death?

In the course of his travels, Ulysses is seen again and again on the edge of an abyss. His adventures with Circe took place close to the abyss. His way on from there led Ulysses literally to the final point, the realm of the dead. And when he meets in the underworld the long procession of mother-figures, he has reached the ultimate roots of mankind. His encounter with Polyphemus, the one-eyed, man-eating giant, also brings Ulysses to a brink. He becomes "No-man," which is the only guise in which he can use his intelligence to escape death. Then, when he has escaped successfully from the cave of the blinded giant, as he gives his real name with pride and a very natural arrogance, the mention of the name brings him once more to the "brink." The angry sea-god Poseidon destroys all the hero's ships and Ulysses is the only survivor. He excapes on a raft of a couple of beams – to the cave of Calypso, the navel and the edge of the sea.

The *Odyssey* would not be one of the great poems of humanity if its hero were not seen again and again on this knife-edge between life and death. Hovering over the void – that was the way of Ulysses, not only as he sailed back from Calypso to Scheria, the land of the Phaeacians, but from its starting point at Troy, as he was carried to Calypso. In the *Odyssey* Homer sings of life as it is pervaded by the constant presence of death. The world of the *Odyssey* is the world of life in suspense, in contact with death, like the right side of a tapestry with the reverse. The yawning depths behind and beneath it are as much part of its make-up as the rest of its being. Ulysses is always suspended over these depths. The sea, the great ambivalent element, is the basic constituent of the abysses and the suspense, the setting of an existential situation which was not Ulysses' alone. Countless Greeks who had listened to the *Odyssey* and to earlier tales and poems about the King of Ithaca's ten-year journey home from Troy were familiar with the situation from their own experience. They were the founders of the Greek colonies, from the Crimea to Spain. The attraction of the unknown, even when it is deadly, and the experience of the terrors of this threat, are the breath of life to discoverers and colonizers.

Much of what we read as we pursue the wanderings of Ulysses is undoubtedly enigmatic and wrapped in a mythical obscurity. But there are so many places where we find exact descriptions of places and events that we cannot but ask ourselves who the writer was. Who was Homer? And could not Homer himself have seen many of the stopping places of his wandering hero?

During excavations carried on by English archaeologists in Ithaca, the homeland of Ulysses, between 1931 and 1953, thirteen bronze three-legged kettles were found in a cave dedicated to the Nymphs and also to Ulysses. The kettles were from the 9th to the 8th century B.C., and the question was asked whether Homer himself had not been there. It cannot be accidental that these thirteen kettles in the Cave of the Nymphs are the exact counterpart of the thirteen kettles given to Ulysses by the Phaeacians, which he hid in a cave after landing. Can it be assumed that Homer was in Ithaca, visited the shrine of the Nymphs and then put the thirteen kettles into his epic?

This question brings up the famous "Homeric problem," which has been debated by scholars for centuries. Was there really one man named Homer behind the two great epics of early Greece, the *Iliad* and the *Odyssey*? Or were these great pieces of literature the product of a collective effort of a number of poets?

The discrepancies which appear in these two great epics, the occasional contradictions and the recurrence of certain refrains, may be explained by the fact that the works were originally oral compositions and hence could and indeed were bound to contain a number of contradictions and weaknesses. It is true that one can hardly overestimate the power of the memory in these epic singers, but one should not go so far as to exclude the occurrence of errors in detail. The refrains or formulas which were a necessary part of the structure of their poems were almost certain to entail errors when they were applied to new contents. The American scholar Milman Parry was the first to investigate the structure of the epic over a broad field in the light of the recurring formulas. Comparison between Homer and south Slav epics, which are still recited from memory, showed astonishing resemblances.

The work of Albert B. Lord, "The Singer of Tales," which appeared after Parry's death, showed that the comparative study of epics allowed Homer to be envisaged as the prototype of epic singers, the greatest master of this genre, who had brought to their supreme perfection the themes which were at his disposal, the prototypes, as it were, of the epic.

We know very little in fact about Homer. He was a poet who lived in the 9th to the 8th century B.C., at the time therefore when the truly Greek culture was beginning to develop in Greece, with the "geometric" type of art. He did not commit his poetry to writing. Like all the poems of the archaic period, they were learned by heart and handed on orally. According to Cicero, it was not till the time of the Athenian "Tyrant" Peisistratus, who died 527 B.C., that the chants of Homer were combined as two epics. The notion that the poet Homer was blind became the established view, because the poet Demodocus among the Phaeacians was also described as blind. The Muse had loved him so much that she gave him the gift of sweet song but left him blind at the same time. This was also supposed to have happened to Homer, and a bust of the 5th century shows him with his closed eyes. But who can be certain that this portrait indicates a blind man and not one who is listening with closed eyes to an inward murmur? It is certain at any rate that this "blindness," in the mind of the Greeks, was a symbol of sublime greatness, signalling a man stamped by his familiarity with the divine. There is also a tradition that Homer, in his old age, conducted a school of poetry on the island of Chios.

This is little enough information, altogether too meager perhaps to convince those who doubt the existence of Homer. But there are two strong arguments in his favor. One is the conviction of the Greeks, who never doubted the existence of their great epic poet. The other is the quality of his poetry. A remark of Aristotle in his *Poetics* about Homer brings out both points clearly, the certainty of his existence and the recognition of the quality of his poetry. Aristotle says of Homer: "He is praiseworthy in many ways, but in particular, he is the only poet who knows when he should speak in his own person in his poetry. The poet himself should have the least to say for himself. He is there to portray and depict. Most other poets hold the stage themselves, and their portrayals are short and few. But Homer introduces a man or a woman or some character without much ado, and all they say and do is characteristic, and not at all out of character." Aristotle's verdict is high praise from an expert, and an apt description of a poet and his work. It would be absurd to suggest that Aristotle meant his verdict to apply to a group of poets.

The achievement of Homer would not indeed have deserved much discussion if it had consisted only in the plan of a great epic and the execution of this plan. The realization of such a plan would have been an achievement, and if done by a poet, the achievement of one with special gifts. But what made Homer's epic the great work that it is was the inward event in the poet in which the world of gods and men was changed.

Homer, who felt himself inspired and transformed by the "Muse," the "goddess," gave humanity a new world view with his two epics, the *Iliad* and the *Odyssey*. One might venture to say, in summing up his special poetic achievement, that in the *Iliad*, the story of the battle of the Greek of the Mycenaean period for Troy, Homer succeeded in "humanizing the divine." The events at Troy had taken place some five hundred years before he wrote, but he brought the stiff and aloof gods of ancient days close to the men of his time. He showed that the inhumanities of war left place for the humane, and he crossed the dividing line between gods and men by making the immortals really take part in the life of man, sympathizing with men and suffering with them. This was a liberating step, by which Homer left far behind him his own times, as depicted in the simplified and stylized forms of geometric art. And his achievement in the *Odyssey* was not less substantial and revolutionary. We can only surmise what poetry was like before the *Iliad*, but it seems that the originality of Homer was that as he told the new and exciting tales which the poet was expected to sing, he also described how gods and men could suffer in war.

In the *Odyssey* Homer takes the opposite route. We might characterize this epic as the "divinization of the human." The story of the sufferings of the sage and wily Ulysses during the ten years of his journey home is more than the adventurous story of a rescued sailor. It is the "mythic picture" of a man who has the force of mind to survive endless adventures and trials on his way home. He finally reaches home, true to himself and his resolve, and so "finds himself." The *Odyssey* has the fascination of a fairy tale, but it also has the atmosphere of a great novel where the reader is absorbed by being caught up into the life and destiny of other men. It was the poet's task to hold men spellbound by strange and eventful tales. But the new achievement of Homer's genius was that he did not confine his art to narrating events. He pictured whole ways of life. We see this again and again in the *Odyssey*. Take for instance the travels of Telemachus. He leaves Ithaca to look for news of his father's fate, guided by Pallas Athene. When he visits the great royal courts of the Mycenaean rulers, the Pylos of the aged King Nestor and the Sparta of Menelaus and Helen, Homer describes for his readers the pomp and luxury of an age already so far past that it is overshadowed by legend. But it is the description of a way of life. So too when he creates once more for the eyes of his readers palace life under the rich Phaeacian king Alcinous, or when he discribes conditions on Ulysses' island, Ithaca, with pictures of country life from the doings of the swineherd Eumaeus or the king's father, Laertes. How strongly this description of ways of life – the element of the novel – predominates in the *Odyssey* may be seen at once from the fact that only four of the twenty-four "books" contain actual accounts of adventures (Books 9–12). Four books are devoted to the journey of Telemachus, four describe life among the Phaeacians after Ulysses' rescue and twelve portray what went on in Ithaca after the Phaeacians had brought Ulysses home.

The predominance of novel-like descriptions of ways of life was a breakthrough in ancient Greek literature. But the structure of the story of the return of Ulysses also reveals the hand of the master with a sovereign command of all the elements of style. The fact that throughout the epic there are two strands of action, which are interwoven in the second part, one concerned with Telemachus and the other with Ulysses, is rather proof of great poetic powers than of the fact that two or more authors were engaged on the work. And in both plots the same basic feeling, the sense of hovering between life and death, is communicated with supreme artistry. Just as the father's way home is constantly menaced, so too the home-coming of the son. His mother's suitors wait in ambush to destroy him.

The *Odyssey*, it might be said, would not be the moving story of a home-coming which it is without this masterly subplot of the journey of Telemachus. It tells the reader exactly what Ulysses is coming home to. It sketches vividly the profile of his wife Penelope and of the son Telemachus whom Ulysses has never seen. It shows finally how necessary was the return of Ulysses to put an end with a strong hand to the rudeness and arrogance of the suitors. The episodes dealing with Telemachus, the description of the faithfulness of Penelope give a new importance to the appeals of Calypso and Nausicaa to win over the sorely tried Ulysses and are the real explanation of his constant yearning for home. Once the reader knows what is happening in Ithaca and how things are moving to a crisis there, with the murderous plot against Telemachus and the mounting pressure on Penelope, the home-coming of Ulysses is a last-minute rescue and the whole action takes on a dramatic tension. Such a drama can only be the creation of *one* poet, an author who is sure of the structure of his work, that is, of Homer.

There is still another special artistic element which reveals the master hand of Homer. Ulysses' home-coming lasted for ten years. If it had been narrated at full epic length it would have been tiresome for the hearers and would finally have become tedious. Aristotle admired the fact that Homer had chosen for the *Odyssey* a single short action and had not tried to describe the whole of the hero's life. As in the *Iliad*, the real action is confined to a few days. It runs from the happy landing of the shipwrecked Ulysses on the island of the Phaeacians to the secret landing a few days later on Ithaca and the fight with the suitors with which the home-coming ends. Nonetheless, the hearer or reader learns all about the adventures at sea, the suitors' efforts to win Ulysses' wife Penelope and her skillful evasion of their wooing over the years. He learns much about the battles for Troy and the fate of the heroes who fought under its walls. Homer succeeds in bringing in effortlessly this mass of material by using the technique of the "reminiscence narrative" – the story within the story. Ulysses tells Alcinous and the Phaeacians of his wanderings; Nestor, Menelaus and Helen tell Telemachus of the Trojan War, the poet Demodocus at the court of Alcinous sings before Ulysses of the trick with the Trojan horse. Then there are the events in Ithaca – the suitors' wooing, their shameless behavior and the faithfulness of Penelope, who unravels by night the threads she has woven by day and so never finishes Laertes' shroud, which she had promised would be the signal for her choice of a suitor – all these events, which precede the actual home-coming, are learned from accounts given by Telemachus, Penelope, and the suitors.

The changes in the form of the narrative allow the poet to deploy his epic at several levels, so that the fairy-tale element and the adventures of the hero recede into the background, while concrete realities like the description of conditions on Ithaca stand out. This realism and strong narrative are the characteristics of Homer's *Odyssey*. In an essay on aesthetics written in the early days of the Roman Empire the *Odyssey* is described as the work of a poet advanced in years. The Greek author writes ("On the Sublime and Beautiful"): "But Homer shows in the *Odyssey* that a great mind, when it is on the wane, takes pleasure in spinning out stories in old age." The *Iliad*, according to the critic, was written "in the full flow of inspiration, while the *Odyssey* is mostly confined to narrative, as befits the wisdom of old age. Hence Homer in the *Odyssey* could be compared to a sinking sun which remains just as great though having lost its glow . . . But like the sea when the tide goes out and its realms are laid bare the ebbing away of Homer's greatness is finally visible, as he wanders to and fro amid the fantastic and incredible. In saying this, I do not forget the tempests of the *Odyssey*, the story of Cyclops and the like. I am speaking of old age, but it is the old age of Homer."

The broad narratives and the switching to and fro which the critic here considers signs of old age, we are rather inclined to regard as particularly modern. And modern critics of Homer attribute the phenomena to the fact that a later poet must have been at work. They also base their doubts as to the Homeric authorship on the presence of several unquestionably weak passages – though there are also similar passages in the *Iliad*. We can understand how they occurred when we recall that these great epics were originally oral compositions into which faults of memory could creep. The great Roman poet Horace dismisses these minor discrepancies in the poems of Homer with a smile when he says: "Even the great Homer sometimes grows drowsy."

Fundamentally, all controversy for or against the existence of Homer and his authorship is futile in view of the sheer quality of the *Iliad* and the *Odyssey* which gives them their supreme place among all Greek poetry. Homer's *Odyssey* is the immortal story of a home-coming, and as the story of a man who follows his path in spite of constant menaces, it is also the story of a man who found himself. The *Odyssey* of Homer is a poem of humanity, completely sketched out and still not wholly finished. Each of us can relive it, and add a new chapter to the tale. This book, which hopes to be a museum of the imagination to help to re-create the Homeric vision of the myth and the Mediterranean, is one such new chapter.

King Priam of Troy asked his daughter-in-law Helen, in the *Iliad*, as he looked out at the hosts of the Greeks besieging Troy: "Who is that man, a head smaller than Agamemnon but broader of shoulders, like a thick-fleeced ram among the sheep?" He was told that it was the wily and inventive Ulysses, King of Ithaca.

Who is Ulysses, the hero of our tale, one of the great figures also in the *Iliad*? If we examine the epithets applied to Ulysses we find that the verdict of his companions wavered between admiration and hate. Sometimes he is called "the offspring of Zeus," "the man of great prudence," "the man who can be matched with Zeus in wisdom" and "the bold of heart." But then Agamemnon describes him as "past-master of evil wiles," "intent on gain," while the hero Achilles despises the "man of many ruses" as one "whose words belie the thoughts he hides within."

Here are thus two aspects to the figure of Ulysses, whom we are to meet in the *Odyssey* as the "godlike sufferer" and of whom the sorceress Circe says: "You have a heart within your breast that cannot be bewitched!" But we also read of the wise and daring Ulysses that "his heart broke" when Circe sent him on his visit to the Underworld and that "he writhed as he wept."

What then is the true Ulysses? One reason for the ambivalence of Ulysses is no doubt that he is a "hero," partly of divine and partly of human descent. But the main reason is that the figure of Ulysses stems from very ancient times, long before the time of Homer and long before even the time of Homer's heroes. At an early stage Ulysses was perhaps a "god." But he was not one of the Olympian gods whom Homer describes. He was rather a daemon, a farmers' god of ancient times, closely linked with the process of nature, its growth and decay. When Ulysses speaks to Penelope of how nature thrives under a good king, he says: "The dark earth bears wheat and barley, the trees are heavy with fruit, the sheep breed constantly, the sea gives fish under the good king, and the people thrive." The words give a glimpse of the nature of the archetypal Ulysses, the mythical nature-god.

Among Etruscan remains we find the mention that Ulysses was "difficult of access" and of a "drowsy nature." How can someone who is always described elsewhere as particularly alert here appear as sleepy? The drowsiness of Ulysses is another pointer to the mythical origin of his figure. Mythical beings sleep, in order not to be disturbed by men. They are inaccessible because they are subject to other laws. And in the *Iliad*, the Ulysses of Homer is also difficult of access. He goes reluctantly to war, as reluctantly in fact as the farmer who has to leave his fields untilled. And many of the wiles of Ulysses may be regarded as peasant cunning, just as the relentless urge of Ulysses to return to Ithaca corresponds to the peasant's longing for his fields. And Ulysses, had he married the bewitching Nausicaa, as the Phaeacians hoped, could have become king in the paradise of Scheria. But he preferred to go back to his homeland, to wring a living from its sparse soil.

But the pre-Homeric myth of the ancestry of Ulysses also contains pointers to the special cunning which could also bring dangers in its train. Ulysses' grandfather is said to be the archthief and robber Autolycus, who in turn is a son of the god Hermes, the god of thieves. But there is more to it than this "hereditary burden" of wiliness and cunning from his grandfather and ancestor. The stories that one told of the master thief Autolycus – the prototypes of the later picaresque novel – also suggest that the archknave Sisyphus, who could challenge Autolycus with his tricks, was the father of Ulysses. Autolycus, we are told, finally came to admire the cunning of Sisyphus so much that he made him his friend and guest, and even offered him his daughter Anticleia, so that he could become the father of the wiliest of the human race. When Laertes, King of Ithaca, was wooing Anticleia, she was already carrying the child of Sisyphus. Homer may not have known this story of Sisyphus' being the father of Ulysses, since he does not give it any mention. Still, the story itself is of interest, since it helps to fill out the picture of Ulysses as it appeared to the Greeks and as it took on new traits age after age.

The usual Greek form of the name Ulysses – Odysseus – is another example of the obscurity which surrounds the hero. Odysseus sounds like a short form of "odyssomenos," the hated. And in the story which tells how the child Odysseus was given his name by his grandfather Autolycus, the archthief and robber says to Laertes and Anticleia: "Give him this name: hated by many came I hither, detested by men and women on this earth our nurse. Odysseus he shall be called." The tale of the giving of the name is simply recognition of the fact that the man of superior cunning and wiles is hated by his fellows, as Autolycus must have known from his own experience. And now we can understand the reproaches brought by Agamemnon and

14

Achilles against Ulysses. They are reproaches which voice their secret hatred of the King of Ithaca, their superior in cunning.

But all this latent sense of the mysterious, hateful, and obscure which clings to the prototype of Ulysses is still only a background in Homer. His Ulysses, the Ulysses we know, is someone else, a more human figure, whose way of acting we can follow even when the gods lend him a hand. He is no longer a mythical power of nature but a palpable figure of flesh and blood. He is a man, an exception no doubt, but subject to all human weaknesses and faults. The fascination of Ulysses, which has held men spellbound for thousands of years, is the way in which he mastered his destiny and the fact that he did so.

The pictures on the following pages show:

1 *The Singer of Tales* – 2 *Pallas Athene, the grey-eyed daughter of Zeus, protectress of Ulysses* – 3 *Ulysses, the inventor of stratagems, King of Ithaca* – 4 *Mount Olympus, the dwelling place of the gods and the holy mountain of Greece* – 5 *Zeus, the father of the gods* – 6 *The sea-god Poseidon who tries to hinder Ulysses' return* – 7 *Athene leaves Olympus and the assembly of the gods, to hasten to Ithaca*

THE ODYSSEY

THE ADVENTURES OF ULYSSES

"O divine poesy, goddess-daughter of Zeus!
Sustain for me this song of the various-minded man
who after he had plundered the inmost citadel of hallowed Troy
was made to stray grievously about the coasts of men,
the sport of their customs good or bad, while his heart
through all the sea-faring ached in an agony to redeem himself
and bring his company safe home." (I, 1–5)

These are the verses with which the poet Homer begins his story of the wanderings and adventures of Ulysses. Of the Greek heroes who had captured and destroyed the city of Troy after ten years' fighting, Ulysses alone, the sage and wily King of Ithaca, has not yet returned to his island home and his wife Penelope. Ulysses has incurred the anger of the sea-god Poseidon, and the lord of the waters pursues him everywhere with his hatred. Driven off course again and again, engaged in battles on unfriendly coasts and battered by tempests, Ulysses has lost all his fleet. His companions are all dead or drowned. He is the only one not swallowed by the waves whipped up by Poseidon, thanks to the protection of the goddess Athene, and he is now cast up on the shore of the island Ogygia. He has been living there for some years. All goes well in appearance because the mistress of the island, the nymph Calypso, shelters the stranded hero in her cave dwelling and heaps favors on him. There is no lack of food and drink and royal garments. The goddess has even besought him again and again to remain on the island as her husband. But Ulysses cannot forget his homeland Ithaca, his beloved Penelope and his son Telemachus. He resists the appeals of the nymph.

THE GODS DEBATE THE HOME-COMING OF ULYSSES

Athene, the divine protectress of Ulysses, has often begged the gods of Olympus to help the home-sick wanderer, and they are finally moved by the hero's sufferings. They meet to take counsel at a moment chosen by the wise Athene, when Ulysses' enemy Poseidon is far from Olympus, at a sacrificial banquet in the land of the Ethiopians. The grey-eyed Athene then tells her father Zeus and the other gods of the privations of the suffering Ulysses, in order to waken their sympathy.

"But my heart is heavy for Ulysses, so shrewd, so ill-fated,
pining in long misery of exile on an island
which is just a speck in the belly of the sea."

(I, 48–50)

Athene succeeds in cajoling her father to decide upon the return of Ulysses. Zeus commands that even Poseidon is now to lay aside his justifiable anger against Ulysses, who had blinded his son, the giant Polyphemus. He also accepts the proposal of Athene, that Hermes, the messenger of the gods, should be sent to the nymph Calypso, to tell the queen of the island that the assembly of the gods has decreed irrevocably the return of Ulysses.

The goddess Athene warmly thanks her father Zeus and the other gods. She herself will now put things in order in Ithaca and have everything ready for the return of its king. She bids farewell to the assembly of the gods on high Olympus with the words:

"For my part I shall go to Ithaca and rouse his son Telemachus,
instilling some tardy purpose into his spirit,
so that he may call his Greek exquisites to council
and give check to the mob of wooers besetting his mother Penelope,
the while they butcher his wealth of juicy sheep
and rolling-gaited, screw-horned oxen.
I will send the youth to Sparta – yes, and to sandy Pylos –
to ask those he meets for news of his dear father's return:
not that he will hear anything, but his zeal
will earn him repute among men."
She ceased, and drew upon her feet
those golden sandals (whose fairness no use could dim)
that carried their mistress as surely and wind-swiftly over the waves
as over the boundless earth. She laid hold of her guardian spear,
great, heavy, and close-grained, tipped with cutting bronze.
When wrath moved the goddess to act, this spear was her weapon:
with it, and stayed by her pride of birth,
she would daunt serried ranks of the very bravest warriors.
Downward she now glided from the summit of Olympus,
to alight on Ithaca before Ulysses' house, by the sill of the main gate.

(I, 88–103)

THE TRAVELS OF TELEMACHUS

Taking the form of Mentes, the Tapian prince friendly to the house of Ulysses, Athene approaches the palace of the hero. For more than three years, ever since hope of the return of the king has been abandoned, a crowd of a hundred and eight suitors with their followers have been living off the possessions of the absent sufferer. They have come from the neighboring islands in the hope of winning the hand of Penelope, the wife of the king now presumed lost, and so attaining royal power. Troubled by their crude importunity, Laertes, the aged father of Ulysses, has withdrawn to his lands. The young son of the king, Telemachus, can only look on helplessly while the suitors make themselves at home in the palace and live high on his and his father's goods. The lovely Penelope still refuses to give her hand in marriage to any of the suitors. But they become more insistent every day. Telemachus tells the whole story to the goddess Athene, whom he has welcomed warmly as an old friend and guest.

20

Athene heard him out and then said fiercely, "A shameful tale!
Here's crying need for Ulysses, to man handle these graceless suitors . . .
Indeed their mating would be bitter and their shrift suddenly sharp.
However such things rest on the knees of the Gods, whose it is to appoint
whether he shall re-enter his halls and exact vengeance, or no.

"Wherefore instead I counsel you to take most earnest thought in what way
you shall by your single self expel the suitors from the house.
Listen to this plan of mine which I would urge upon you . . .
Get yourself a ship of twenty rowers, the very best ship you can find.
Set forth in this to seek news of your long-overdue father.
Even if no mortal tells you anything, yet who knows but there may steal
into your mind that divine prompting by which Zeus very often
gives mankind an inkling of the truth. Go to Pylos first and consult
its revered Nestor; thence to Sparta where you will find brown-haired
Menelaus, latest of all the mail-clad Achaeans to get back from Troy.
If you learn that your father is living and has his face towards home,
then steel your temper to one more year of this afflicted house.
But if you learn that he is no more – that he is surely dead –
then return and throw up a mound to his name, with the plenishing
and ceremonial befitting a great fallen warrior: after which
do you yourself give his widow, your mother, to some man for wife.

"These things first. Yet also it must be your study and passion
to slay these suitors in your house, either by fair fight or by
stratagem. Childishness no longer beseems your years:
you must put it it away."

(I, 252–254, 266–270, 279–297)

Having thus strengthened the young man's courage, the goddess takes flight, in the form of a bird. Telemachus suddenly realizes that he has been visited by a god in human form.

Meanwhile the suitors are banqueting in the royal hall of Ulysses and drinking his wine. Finally they call for the poet Phemius to entertain them. He sings to the tipsy men of the sad home-coming of the Greeks from Troy. And his singing saddens above all the heart of the mournful Penelope, who hears the song in the women's quarters and is reminded once more of the Ulysses who is always close to her heart. With tears in her eyes, she hastens to the banqueting-hall to forbid the singer to go on. Telemachus, however, encouraged by the promise of the goddess, goes to his mother and soothes her.

"We have no cause against Phemius for drawing music out of the hard
fate of the Danaans. A crowd ever extols the song which sounds
freshest in its ears. Harden your heart and mind to hear this tale.
Remember that Ulysses was not singular in utterly losing at Troy
the day of his return. There were others, many others, who in the Troad
lost their very selves. Wherefore I bid you get back to your part
of the house, and be busied in your proper sphere, with the loom and the spindle,

and in overseeing your maids at these, their tasks.
Speech shall be the men's care: and principally my care:
for mine is the mastery in this house."

(I, 350–359)

Then Telemachus turns on the carousing suitors, calls them to order and announces that he is going to convoke a council for the next morning, at which they will be publicly summoned to leave his house at last. The suitors listen with anger and astonishment to the resolute words of the young man.

Telemachus gets up the next morning with new strength and orders the heralds to call the men of Ithaca to an assembly. His face shines with a heavenly grace bestowed upon him by Athene, and the whole people are transfixed with astonishment. He seizes the royal scepter and denounces the ill-mannered intruders in a fiery speech, where he tells how they have been living for more than three years in the house of his father Ulysses, devouring his provisions and burdening his mother with their importunate wooing. When he finally throws the scepter angrily to the ground there is not a movement in the crowd and for the moment no one dares to contradict the king's son.

But then the boldest of the suitors, Antinous, springs up and defends his conduct and that of his companions. The suitors, Antinous cries, are not the cause of the long delay, but Penelope. She had promised to choose one of the suitors as soon as she had woven the windingsheet for the aged Laertes, Ulysses' father. But Penelope has fooled them all for three years. She unravels secretly at night as much of the shroud as she has woven each day.

"We shall not go about our business nor go home till she
has made her choice and been married to some one of us Achaeans."

(II, 128–129)

The obdurate Antinous ends his speech with these words, having summoned Telemachus to order his mother to make her choice at last. And he is to send her home to her father's house, where the marriage is to be celebrated.

Telemachus of course refuses to yield to the bold demands of the suitors. And Zeus sends him and the assembly two eagles which fight over the heads of the crowd and then soar away to the right over the city. One of the ancients interprets this as an ominous sign for the suitors. But they only laugh. "There are many birds flying under the sun, but they are not all omens," says one of the suitors, affirming that they will still go on carousing in the palace of Ulysses till Penelope has made her decision.

In this situation Telemachus prudently refuses to continue the debate. But he now demands of the gathering, as Athene has advised him, to supply him with a ship with twenty oarsmen, so that he can travel from place to place inquiring after the fate of his parent. But the suitors only laugh at the young man's plan. Telemachus goes to the seashore and begs the help of Pallas Athene, which is then promised him. She mingles with the crowd in the guise of the aged Mentor and wins twenty volunteers for Telemachus' voyage. Then she makes the suitors drunk, to prevent their noticing the young man's departure, and brings him to the ship, which has in the meantime been provisioned for the journey.

Afterwards Telemachus went on board (Athene having preceded him)
and sat down in the stern-sheets, quite near where she had seated herself.
The crew loosed the after-warps, clambered aboard,
and took their seats on the oar-benches.

Then did Athene, the clear-eyed, summon up for them a favouring breeze,
a brisk following west wind which thrummed across the wine-dark sea.
Telemachus roused his followers and bade them get sail on the vessel.
They obeyed him: the fir mast was raised aloft and heeled
through its pierced cross-beams: the stays were rigged
and the white sails hauled up by their halyards
of pliant cowhide. The wind caught the sail, bellying it out,
and the blue-shadowed waves resounded under the fore-foot
of the running ship as she lay over on her course
and raced out to sea.

(II, 417–430)

WITH KING NESTOR IN PYLOS

Forth from the lovely waters sprang the sun
into its firmament of brass, thence to shine upon the Immortals,
as also upon mortal men walking amid the corn-fields of earth;
while the ship drew into Pylos, the stately citadel of Neleus.
There upon the fore-shore were gathered the inhabitants,
doing sacrifice to the Earth-shaker, Poseidon, the dark-tressed God.

(III, 1–6)

. . . they encountered the throng of the men of Pylos.
There sat Nestor amongst his sons,
with his followers busied about him, arranging the feast
or roasting joints of beef or skewering choice morsels on the spits.
Yet no sooner did they spy strangers than one and all
crowded forward with welcoming hands,
to have them take place in the gathering.
Peisistratus, Nestor's son, reached them first.
He took a hand of Athene and a hand of Telemachus
and led them to fleecy sheepskins
spread over the sand of the beach beside the platters . . .

(III, 31–37)

During the meal Telemachus now asks the wise Nestor about his father Ulysses. And Nestor
tells him of the battles of the Greeks before Troy, and of the homeward journey which was so
troublesome for many. He then tells of the quarrel between the two leaders, Agamemnon and
Menelaus, and how Agamemnon met a dreadful death in his fortress of Mycenae and how his son

Orestes took vengeance on the adulterous mother. But then Nestor advises Telemachus to go to Sparta to see King Menelaus, whose home-coming from Troy had also been delayed. He promises him horses and chariots to bring him safely to Sparta under the guidance of his sons. But he invites him to spend the night in his palace. Athene, in the guise of Mentor, accepts the invitation on behalf of Telemachus, while she herself, as she says, will stay by the ship overnight.

The goddess ended her say, and took flight from them,
in the way of a sea-eagle. Astonishment fell on all present
and the venerable man was awed at what his eyes saw.
He seized Telemachus by the hand, crying his name and saying:
"Friend Telemachus, what fear could one have
of your growing up weak or base, when from your youth
gods walk with you as guides? Of the great dwellers on Olympus
this can be no other than the Daughter of Zeus himself:
the Tritonian, the all-glorious: who also was wont to single out
your great father for honour, from among the Argives." (III, 371–379)

The next morning, Nestor offers a solemn sacrifice in honor of Athene. He chooses an unblemished cow as victim and in honor of the goddess has its horns covered with sparkling gold. While Nestor and his men are preparing for the festive sacrificial meal outside, Telemachus remains in the palace and is cared for by young maidservants.

During this sacrifice beautiful Polycaste,
the youngest grown daughter of Nestor son of Neleus,
had given Telemachus his bath, washing him and anointing him with rich olive oil
before she draped him in a seemly tunic and cloak:
so that he came forth from the bath-cabinet with the body of an immortal.
He rejoined Nestor, the shepherd of his people . . . (III, 464–469)

Then, when all had enjoyed the banquet, Nestor orders the horses to be yoked so that Telemachus can be on his way. The journey, which takes the two royal princes from the coast to Sparta in the interior, lasts two days. Toward the evening of the second day, after passing through luxuriant fields of wheat, they reach in the valley the great city and the fortress of Menelaus.

WITH MENELAUS AND HELEN IN SPARTA

The two princes, Telemachus the son of Ulysses and Peisistratus the son of Nestor, are made welcome in the palace. When they have cleaned away the dust of the journey and been dressed for the feast, they are brought by the servants to the banqueting hall of the citadel, where King Menelaus is celebrating along with a large number of guests the double engagement of his son and of his daughter. When the two new guests have eaten and drunk, Menelaus, like King Nestor, tells of the various blows of fate which befell the Greek heroes after the end of the battle for Troy. He laments above all the treacherous killing of his brother Agamemnon. Then he goes on to say:

The pictures on the following pages show:

"Yet above and beyond all my company do I especially vex my weeping
heart for ONE, whose memory makes me utterly loathe sleep and food.
No man of the Achaeans deserved so greatly or laboured
so greatly as great Ulysses laboured and endured.
For him it was written that the outcome should be
but sorrow upon sorrow: and for me a distress for his sake
not ever to be forgotten while he continues missing
and we in ignorance of whether he be alive or dead.
Without doubt they mourn him too, old Laertes
and self-possessed Penelope and Telemachus,
who was no more than a child newly-born,
left behind by his father in the house."
    Thus he spoke, and his words moved in the son a longing
to bewail his father when he heard mention of his name.
A tear splashed from his eyelids to the ground
and he lifted up the purple cloak with both hands before his eyes:
while Menelaus who noted it guessed the significance . . .
                              (IV, 104–116)

At that moment, Helen enters the banqueting hall. She is still of incomparable beauty, the
woman for whose sake the Trojan War broke out, when Paris, the son of the King of Troy,
abducted the lovely Helen from Sparta and made her his wife. Accompanied by her maidservants,
who carry the golden spindle given her long ago by the Queen of Thebes in the land of Egypt,
Helen passes along the hall and sits down on the royal throne beside her husband Menelaus. Then
she looks at the weeping Telemachus and says with astonishment to Menelaus: "I have never
seen anyone so like a son of the noble Ulysses as this young man." Menelaus, too, as he tells Helen,
had been struck by the amazing resemblance of Telemachus to Ulysses. And then the son of King
Nestor addresses Menelaus with the words:

"Menelaus, Zeus-fostered son of Atreus,
leader of the common people, my friend here is indeed the son of that man,
the one and only, as you say."
                              (IV, 156–157)

And Peisistratus goes on to tell of Telemachus' difficulties with the hordes of suitors who are
devouring his possessions at home in Ithaca. Menelaus recalls once more all the heroes of Troy,
but above all the noble Ulysses, whom he would so gladly have as his friend and neighbor,
if only he had returned home. To cheer the sad company, Helen puts a philtre in the wine which
banishes all cares. And while the men are enjoying the delicacies of the banquet, Queen Helen
begins to speak of Ulysses:

"Touching a single one of those innumerable adventures of Ulysses;
one only, for beyond all my listing or telling were the exploits of
that hardy one. Marvellous was this adventure which the iron-nerved

25

man conceived and dared to execute in the Troad of unhappy memory
to all Achaeans. He punished himself with humiliating stripes
and threw a coarse wrap about his shoulders as if he were
a bondsman: and so went down into the broad streets of the hostile
city amongst his enemies, hiding himself in his foreign shape
and making believe he was a mendicant, a figure very unlike
that he cut in the Achaean fleet. Yet in this disguise
he went through the city of the Trojans – and not a soul of them
accosted him. But I knew who this man was and challenged him
again and again while he cunningly eluded my questions.
After the washing and anointing with oil when I was
clothing him in new garments I swore to him a mighty oath
that I would not declare to the Trojans that it was Ulysses,
before he had got back to the swift ships and the bivouacs.
Then he told me all the intention of the Achaeans . . ."

(IV, 240–256)

Menelaus and Helen recount together the story of the Trojan horse, invented by the wily Ulysses for the conquest of Troy.

The next morning Telemachus asks Menelaus for any news he may have of the whereabouts of his father Ulysses. And Menelaus tells him of the prophecy of the sea-god Proteus, whom he had taken captive on the strand of Egypt on his way home from Troy and forced to give information about the other Greek princes. Proteus had spoken of Ulysses as follows:

"The son of Laertes, the lord of Ithaca, I saw him in an island
letting fall great tears throughout the domain of the nymph
Calypso who there holds him in constraint: and he may not
get thence to his own land, for he has by him no oared ships
or company to bear him across the sea's great swell." (IV, 555–560)

Telemachus now knows at least that his father is alive, and he is eager to go home to Ithaca. Menelaus invites him to spend a few more days as his guest at Sparta, but Telemachus declines, and sets off for home with a rich present from the king, a mixingbowl from the workshop of the divine metalworker Hephaestos.

THE SUITORS' MURDEROUS PLOT

At Ithaca in the meantime the suitors have learned by accident that the young Telemachus has in fact launched out on his voyage of inquiry into the fate of his father. When they had not seen him for a few days, they thought he was gone to the country to see after the herds. Now they are beside themselves with rage when they learn that Telemachus has had his way. Antinous again makes himself the spokesman of his companions and cries out in anger:

"I ask you to supply me a fast ship and a crew of twenty men,
with which to watch and waylay him as he comes
through the narrow gut between Ithaca and steep Samos:
that this gadding about after his father may cost him dear at last." (IV, 669–671)

The other suitors accept the plan of murder with enthusiasm. And the news of the crime which
is planned spreads rapidly throughout the city and the palace. Penelope learns of it from the loyal
herald Medon, who detests the suitors. The queen's heart trembles when she hears the news, and
her eyes fill with tears. Her maidservants weep with her, and the vivacious nurse Eurycleia only
succeeds gradually in soothing her.

But then Penelope prays to the goddess Athene, and when she finally sleeps, worn out by care,
the goddess appears to her in the form of a friendly princess and speaks consoling words about the
destiny of Telemachus:

"Be brave: give not fear too large rule over your heart.
There goes with him a guide of power such as all men
would pray to have stand by them, even Pallas Athene.
She takes mercy upon your grief and directly sends me
that I may speak to you these comforts." (IV, 825–829)

Penelope wakes next morning comforted and strengthened by the promise of the goddess,
which in the light of morning appeared as a meaningful dream.

While this was happening to Penelope, the suitors had not delayed to put their ruthless plan
into action. In the afternoon, a fast ship had been fitted out and laden with provisions. Then,
in the darkness, a crew of twenty men had embarked and sailed secretly out of the harbor, heading
for the place of ambush where they meant to fall upon the young Telemachus at his return.

The suitors set forth, harbouring sudden death for Telemachus
in their hearts, and sailed the waterways as far as a stony
island in mid-sea, equidistant from Ithaca and craggy Samos . . . (IV, 842–845)

THE GODS DECREE THE HOME-COMING OF ULYSSES

On Olympus, the towering mountain of the gods, the Immortals have gathered once more to
take counsel about the fate of Ulysses. Once more Athene beseeches her father Zeus and the
other gods to have pity at last on the patient Ulysses. She cries out in anger:

"Divine Ulysses was a clement and fatherly king; but no one
of the men, his subjects, remembers it of him for good:
while fate has abandoned him to languish sorely
in Lady Calypso's island, kept there by her high hand,
a prisoner in her house. Nor has he power to regain

the land of his fathers, seeing that he lacks galleys
and followers to speed him over the broad back of ocean.
Moreover, there is now a plot afoot to murder his darling
son as he returns from sacred Pylos or noble Lacedaemon,
whither he went in hope to hear somewhat of his father."

(V, 11–20)

Zeus, the gatherer of the clouds, calms his daughter. He reminds her that the gods have already determined, when they last took counsel, to put an end to the sufferings of Ulysses. And the gods have already agreed on the fate of the shameless wooers of Penelope. Ulysses is to put them to death on his return. Zeus therefore bids Athene to see to the safe return of Telemachus. But he commands Hermes, the messenger of the gods, to go quickly to the island of Ogygia and announce to the nymph Calypso the decree of the gods. She must now free Ulysses and concern herself with his home-coming.

Hermes seizes his herald's staff, draws on his winged shoes of gold, and storms down from Olympus to speed over the sea.

But when at last he attained that remote island, he quitted
the purple sea and went inland as far as the great cave
in which lived the nymph of the well-braided hair.
He chanced to find her within . . .

In the cavern he did not find great-hearted Ulysses,
who sat weeping on the shore as was his wont,
crying out his soul with groaning and griefs
and letting flow his tears while he eyed the fruitless sea.

(V, 59–62, 81–84)

The nymph Calypso welcomes the winged messenger of the gods, regales him with nectar and ambrosia, the food of the gods, and asks him what is the reason for his visit. Hermes announces the decision of the gods about the home-coming of Ulysses.

The nymph complains bitterly. "You are the most cruel of all, O gods," she cries, "and envious of heart," and reminds the divine messenger of other cases in which the Immortals had thwarted the love of a goddess for a mortal man. But she obeys the command of Zeus and promises to help Ulysses with her advice for a happy homeward journey.

She finds the resourceful Ulsysses on the seacoast, staring sadly at the waters, and tells him of the decree of the gods. Then she bids him make a raft to take him home. The nymph and Ulysses take one more meal together and she tries again to make the hero stay with her, comparing her own beauty with that of Penelope. But Ulysses answers steadfastly:

"O Queen and Divinity, hold this not against me.
In my true self I do most surely know
how far short of you discreet Penelope falls
in stature and comeliness. For she is human:
and you are changeless, immortal, ever-young.

Yet even so I choose – yea all my days are consumed
in longing – to travel home and see the day
of my arrival dawn. If a god must shatter me
upon the wine–dark sea, so be it. I shall suffer
with a high heart; for my courage has been tempered
to endure all misery. Already have I known
every mood of pain and travail, in storms and in the war.
Let the coming woe be added to the count of those which have been."

(V, 215–224)

Ulysses builds his craft in four days with the help of the divine Calypso. On the morning of the fifth day he launches out with the wind filling his sail and heads away to sea. For seventeen days the mild wind which the nymph sends him carries him along. On the morning of the eighteenth day he catches sight in the distance of the mountains of the land of the Phaeacians. The exhausted hero already feels that he has reached safety.

But then Poseidon, on his way back from the land of the Ethiopians, perceives Ulysses' raft. He is filled with rage as he recognizes that the other gods have taken advantage of his absence to secure the return of Ulysses. And now the Lord of the Seas stirs up the floods with his trident, commands the hurricanes to blow and the mighty waves to tower. Earth and sky are swallowed up in the dark clouds which the sea-god has gathered in his anger, to destroy Ulysses.

Under the fury of the waves, first the mast of Ulysses' raft is brought down, then the rudder is torn from his hand, and finally he himself is washed overboard. But he does not give up the struggle. Dizzy from the beating of the waves, he comes up once more, uses his last ounce of strength to swim to the raft and even succeeds in clambering on board. Hanging on to his raft, he is driven to and fro by wind and wave like a shuttlecock, till the sea-goddess Leucothea espies him and takes pity on his misery. She rises out of the foaming waves, seats herself on the craft beside the helpless victim and advises him to cast away his clothes and swim for safety to the neighboring shore of the Phaeacians. She also gives him a sacred veil in which to wrap himself.

No sooner has the goddess dived once more into the sea than Poseidon sends a mountainous wave which crashes down on Ulysses' craft and breaks it in pieces. He straddles a beam, wraps the magic veil about him, and then plunges courageously into the raging waves. For two days and two dreadful nights the victim of Poseidon's anger is tossed about the sea. Finally, as the rosy light of the third day is dawning the wind dies down and the sea becomes smooth. Close by, Ulysses sees the shore which means rescue.

But the coast towards which the sorely tried hero is being driven is abrupt. The waves break in thunder on the steep rocks. Ulysses recognizes that no one could find safety here. He would be dashed to pieces against the cliffs. So he swims on until under the guidance of his protectress the goddess Athene he reaches a bay with a gently sloping shore, where a little river falls into the sea. Ulysses uses the last of his strength to swim to land and sinks down in a faint.

When after a long period of exhaustion his emergency returns, Ulysses first unwraps from his shoulders the veil of the sea-goddess which has helped him so well and casts it back in the sea, as the goddess had commanded him. Then he kisses thankfully the ground of his rescue and looks about him for a place where he can find protection for the night. And he sees two great olive trees with their branches intertwined.

So closely did they grow together and supplement each other
that through them no force of moist winds could pierce:
nor could the shining of the sun cast in any ray;
nor would any downpour of rain soak through.
    Beneath them did Ulysses creep, and set to scraping together
with his own hands a broad bed for himself:
for inside there had drifted such a pile of dry leaves
as would have covered two or three men
well enough for a winter-time, however hard the weather.
When bold Ulysses saw the leaves he rejoiced and laid himself down in the midst of them
and fell to pouring the litter by handfuls over his body, till he was covered.

                                          (V, 480–487)

ULYSSES AND NAUSICAA

While Ulysses sleeps exhausted under the protecting olive trees, Athene has gone to the city
of the Phaeacians to take further steps for the safety of her protégé. Entering the palace of King
Alcinous, she goes to the bedroom of the king's daughter Nausicaa, a girl who could match the
Immortals in beauty and spirit. In the guise of one of Nausicaa's companions Athene approaches
the sleeping girl and says to her:

    "O Nausicaa, how careless has your mother's daughter grown!
These rich clothes all lie neglected . . .
Therefore let us go washing tomorrow at the break of day."

                                          (VI, 25–26, 31)

    At this, the lovely Nausicaa awakes from her sleep and wonders at her dream. But then she
hastens to her father, King Alcinous, and asks him for a chariot and a yoke of mules, to take her
and her companions to the river, to wash the clothes of the royal house. When the chariot is
ready, the girls drive to the bank of the river, unyoke the animals, and wash the clothes in friendly
rivalry.

    Afterward, when all the dirt was worked right out,
they stretched the linen wide and smooth upon the foreshore,
even on the pure shingle where the sea had washed it clean.
    The work being done they fell to bathing, and then anointed
themselves to sleekness with their olive oil before carrying
their provisions to a nook which overlooked the sea;
where they ate and waited as the clothes lay out
in the sunlight drying. The food having satisfied
their appetites the hand-maids and their young mistress
next threw off their scarves and turned to playing with a ball. (VI, 93–100)

Finally, the girls prepare to go home. But Athene, the blue-eyed daughter of heavenly Zeus, is considering how she can awaken Ulysses from his sleep, so that he will see the lovely Nausicaa, and Nausicaa can bring him to the city of the Phaeacians. She makes Nausicaa throw the ball once more to one of the players. But the ball, diverted by the goddess, misses the girl and falls into the swirling river. The girls scream, and their cries waken Ulysses, where he is sleeping under the olive trees nearby.

Drunken with sleep, Ulysses first fears that he has been cast up on a shore inhabited by barbarians and inhuman robbers. But then he takes courage.

"By the voices I do think them human. Let me go forward,
and if I can see . . ." Thus muttering Ulysses crept out
from his bushes, snapping off in his powerful hands
from the thick tree one leafy shoot with which to shield
from sight the maleness of his body. So he sallied forth,
like the mountain-bred lion exulting in his strength . . .
  So boldly did Ulysses, stark naked as he was,
make to join the band of maidens: for necessity compelled him.
None the less he seemed loathsome in their sight
because of his defilement with the sea-wrack;
and in panic they ran abroad over all the spits of the salt beaches.
Only the daughter of Alcinous remained;
for Athene had put courage into her heart
and taken terror from her limbs
so that she stood still, facing him. (VI, 125–130, 135–141)

He begins by singing the praises of the beauty of the princess. Then he tells her that he has been shipwrecked and tossed about by the seas for days. He asks her for help, and Nausicaa gladly agrees. She tells him that he is in the land of the Phaeacians and that she herself is the king's daughter.

Then she calls her companions, and at their mistress's summons, the frightened girls return hesitatingly. Nausicaa orders them to wash the stranger in the river, to bring oils to anoint him and clothes to cover him. But Ulysses puts the girls aside. With his own hands he washes the crusted salt from his arms and shoulders and rubs away the foam of the stormy sea from his head. And then Athene, when the hero has anointed himself with fragrant oil and clad himself in tunic and mantle, lends him a radiant beauty. When he approaches Nausicaa, she regards him with astonishment. She speaks:

"Hush now and listen, my white-armed attendants, while I speak.
Not all the gods inhabiting Olympus have opposed
the entering in of this man among the sanctified Phaeacians.
At first he appeared to me not a seemly man: but now he is
like the gods of spacious heaven. O that such a man
might settle contentedly in our city, and agree to be called my husband!
But come now, women, give the stranger food and drink." (VI, 238–246)

When Ulysses, who had had no food for days, has been regaled with food and drink, Nausicaa mounts the chariot. She tells the stranger to follow her and the girls until they reach the grove of Athene. There he is to wait alone, while the girls go on to the nearby city of Alcinous. The lovely daughter of the king does not wish to set gossips talking. It must not be thought that she has sought a bridegroom in foreign lands, as they might say if she returned home in the company of a handsome stranger. Ulysses is to let some time elapse, and only then, when the chariot has reached the city, is he to leave the grove and make for the king's palace. And there he is not to begin by greeting the king. He must first clasp the knees of the queen and beg for help.

"If only my mother favours your impression in her heart
you may hope to see your friends and come
to your stately home and fatherland."
                    (VI, 313–315)

Ulysses follows Nausicaa's orders. He remains behind in the grove and before making for the palace of Alcinous, he prays to the goddess Athene:

"Hear me, Unwearied One, child of Zeus who holds the Aegis.
Especially I pray you now to hear me,
forasmuch as you did not lately when I was broken –
when there broke me the famous Earth-shaker.
Give me to find love and pity among the Phaeacians."
    So he prayed. Pallas Athene heard him . . .
                    (VI, 324–328)

ULYSSES AMONG THE PHAEACIANS

Having given the divinely beautiful Nausicaa the start she asked for on her way to the city, Ulysses himself sets out. But Athene, fearing that one of the proud Phaeacians might offer offense to the stranger, wraps her favorite in the darkness of night, so that he reaches the city without being seen. There Athene appears to him in the guise of a Phaeacian girl, and leads him at his request to the palace of Alcinous. Full of astonishment, Ulysses observes the luxuriant paradise of the royal gardens, admires the magnificence of the lofty palace, and sees from the number of servants about that the owner must indeed be rich. When they reach the entrance of the royal hall, his guide Athene leaves the hero, and advises him, as Nausicaa had already done, to begin by throwing himself on the mercy of the queen, Arete.
    Still invisible to human eyes, Ulysses passes through the great hall to the thrones of the royal couple. There at last Athene dissipates the cloud which hides him, lending the stranger now visible a beauty like that of the Immortals. While the Phaeacians, who have just ended their feast and are about to retire to rest, look on with astonishment, Ulysses clasps the queen's knees and cries out:

32

The pictures on the following pages show:

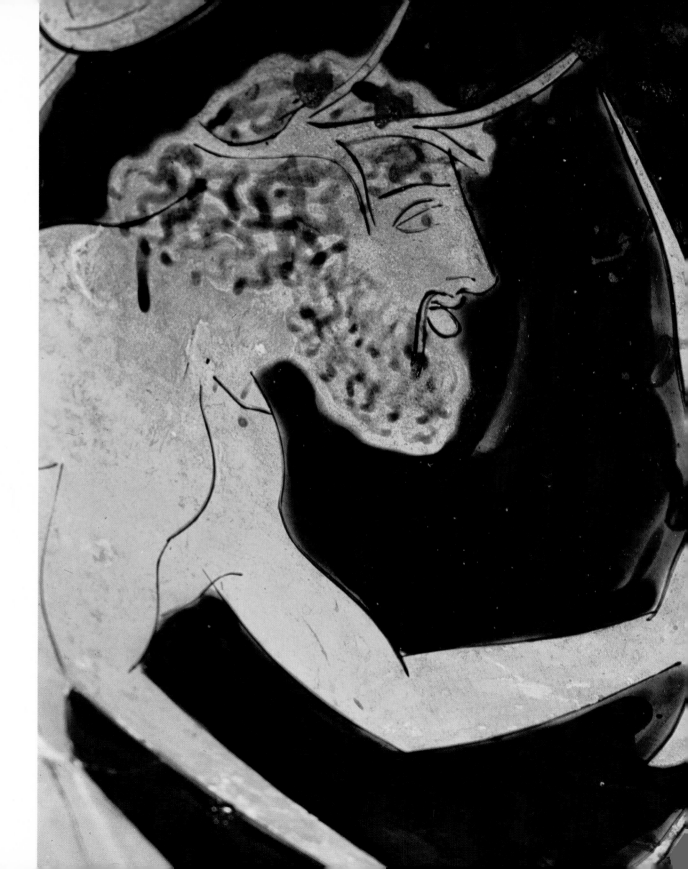

"O Arete, daughter of godlike Rhexenor, to your husband
and to your knees I come, in my extremity. And to these guests too.
May the gods give them happiness, while they live; and permit
each to hand down his goods and houses to his children,
together with such consideration as the world has rendered him.
But for me, I pray you, hasten my despatch by the quickest way
to my native place. Now for so long have I been sundered
from my friends and in torment." After speaking
he crouched down on the hearth among the ashes of the fire:
and for a time the hall was very still. (VII, 146–154)

Then the oldest of the Phaeacian nobles demanded that the king should not leave the stranger
to sit in the ashes, but welcome him hospitably, as was the custom. And the king takes Ulysses
by the hand and leads the resourceful hero to a seat by his throne making his dear son Laodamos
give place. And while the servants bring the stranger food and drink, the king, without asking
his guest what is his name and where he comes from, promises him a safe ship the next day to
bear him to his home.

Queen Arete, however, has noticed that the stranger's clothes come from her household
and asks him what has happened. And the wily Ulysses tells of his stay on the island of Ogygia
where the nymph Calypso kept him captive for over seven years, until she was forced by the
command of Zeus to let him go. He then describes his dreadful shipwreck, his landing on the
Phaeacian coast, and his meeting with the lovely Nausicaa. Both Alcinous and Queen Arete
agree that their daughter had acted rightly. And Alcinous, pleased by the wise and eloquent
discourse of his guest, even invites him to remain permanently as his son-in-law. Alcinous says:

"Ah me! by Zeus the Father and Athene and Apollo!
Would there might be found some man like you,
my double in niceness and sentiment, to accept
my daughter and the name of my son-in-law, and to live here for good.
It would delight me to provide house and property, if you would stay!
Yet fear not that any one of us Phaeacians will detain you here by
foul means. It would not be pleasing in the sight of Zeus.
On the contrary, that you may know for certain, I shall here and now
fix the day of your going. Tomorrow, let it be.
Tomorrow you shall lie down and slumber soundly,
while the oars of your crew smite the smooth sea,
bringing you all the way to your land and house, those things you love."
(VII, 311–320)

After this repeated promise of the king, all retire to rest. And the next morning, the king
convokes an assembly of the people in the market place. Ulysses, still enhanced by Athene with
superhuman stature and divine beauty, is the admiration of all as he takes his place beside the king.
When the crowd, whom Athene has filled with enthusiasm, is fully gathered, the king orders
a new ship to be fitted out for the stranger's homeward voyage. Twenty-five young nobles

are to make ready to bring the noble castaway to his home, speeding him on his way with their oars. Then Alcinous invites all the nobles to a farewell feast in the palace, where twelve sheep, eight pigs, and two oxen have been slaughtered and prepared.

In the course of the banquet, the singer Demodocus, to whom the Muse gave the gift of sweet song, but took instead the light of his eyes, raises his voice to sing of the heroes of Troy and the quarrel between Achilles and Agamemnon. As the stranger listens, he covers his face with his mantle, so that the guests should not see his tears. Alcinous alone notices the grief of his guest and orders games to be held in order to entertain him. The noblest youths of the Phaeacians then compete with each other, at running, jumping, wrestling, boxing, and throwing the discus, in honor of their guest. Finally, Laodamos, the king's favorite son, invites the stranger to take part in the games. But Ulysses refuses, because he is more concerned at the moment with his grief than with the games. One of the young Phaeacians, disappointed at the refusal, speaks harshly to Ulysses, calling him a traveling salesman, with nothing of the hero or warrior about him. The noble Ulysses grows indignant, turns on the speaker and says:

"Your reviling made the heart beat faster in my breast.
I am no ninny at sports, as you would have it. Indeed
I think I was among the best, in my time, while I yet heard
the prompting of my youth and hands. In my time – for here
I subsist in pain and misery, having risked and endured
much in the wars of men and the wearisome seas.
Yet despite the ravages of these evil things I will essay
your tests of strength: for that sneer galled me
and your word has stung me to the quick."
He spoke and sprang to his feet. All cloaked as he was
he seized a throwing weight, a huge heavy stone far bigger
than those with which the Phaeacians had been competing.
He whirled it up and flung it from his mighty hand,
and the stone sang through the air. Down they quailed to
the earth, those Phaeacians of the long oars, those master mariners,
beneath the hurtling of the stone which soared so freely
from the hero's hand that it overpassed the marks of every other.

(VIII, 178–193)

After this throw, which left the Phaeacians amazed, the stranger challenges the youths to compete with him, at whatever sport they choose. He claims himself to be most skillful at archery. But none of the Phaeacians responds.

Then the king soothes the hero and excuses the irritating words of the youth. To reconcile the stranger, he orders the youths to perform their dances, singly and in groups, for his enjoyment. Ulysses admires the incomparable dancers, and praises them to the king. And the king, to blot out entirely the offense to his guest, makes the twelve princes of the people bring him rich presents. Each offers a cloak, a tunic, and also a talent of the finest gold. The king himself adds similar gifts, and the young man, Euryalus, who spoke the offensive words, gives the

34

stranger a magnificently wrought sword with an ivory sheath. The queen places all these gifts in a chest for the hero, and then Ulysses himself, at her invitation, fastens the box with cunning knots.

After a refreshing bath, Ulysses rejoins the Phaeacians in the banqueting hall for a farewell meal. At the threshold of the hall he is met again by the divine Nausicaa, who says to him:

"Farewell, Stranger; and when in your native land think of me, sometimes:
for it is chiefly to me that you owe the gage of your life."
Ulysses answered her, saying, "Nausicaa, daughter of high-souled Alcinous:
if Zeus, Hera's Lord, the Thunderer, wills that I reach home
and see the day of my return, there and then I will pay vows to you,
as to a divine one: and for ever and ever throughout my days.
For you gave me life, Maiden."
He ended and passed to his throne beside King Alcinous.
                                    (VIII, 461–469)

For the farewell meal, the noble singer Demodocus was also led back to the royal hall. Ulysses cuts for him a special portion of the roast and has it carried to him. At the end of the meal the resourceful Ulysses then addresses the singer with the words:

"Demodocus, I laud you above all mortal men:
I know not if it was the Muse, daughter of Zeus, that taught you,
or Apollo himself. Anyhow you have sung the real history
of the mishaps of the Achaeans, their deeds, their sufferings, their griefs,
as if you had been there or had heard it from eye-witnesses.
But now change your theme and sing
of how Epeius with the help of Athene carpentered together
that great timber horse, the crafty device,
which wise Ulysses got taken into the citadel
after packing it with the men who were to lay Troy waste."
                                    (VIII, 487–495)

Then the singer recounts to the attentive Phaeacians the story of the Trojan horse. But tears spring again to Ulysses' eyes as he hears the tale. And though he succeeds once more in hiding his grief from the other guests, the noble Alcinous again remarks it. He bids the poet to be silent, because his song disturbs his guest. Then he turns once more to the stranger, who is as dear to him as his brother, and asks him:

"Tell us by what name they call you there at home –
your mother and father and the others in your city and district.
For all parents fit names to their children as soon as these are born,
so that there is no one so poor or so gentle that he is nameless.
Tell me your land and district and city, that our sentient ships
may get their bearing for your journey." (VIII, 550–556)

THE ADVENTURES OF ULYSSES

When Ulysses is thus requested by King Alcinous, not out of importunate curiosity but friendly sympathy, he finally answers him, having first praised once more the artistry of the singer. And the resourceful traveler makes himself known, saying:

"I am Ulysses, son of Laertes; a name which among men spells
every resource and subtlety of mind: and my fame reaches heaven.
I live in pellucid Ithaca . . ." (IX, 19–21)

As King Alcinous and the wondering Phaeacians listen, Ulysses then begins the story of his sad journey homewards from Troy.

His misfortunes begin, he tells them, immediately after his departure. A favorable wind bears his ships to the city of Ismaros in the land of the Cicones. The city is conquered and destroyed, and the attack is rewarded by rich booty. But against Ulysses' advice, his companions celebrate the victory, and the scattered Cicones can re-form and fall upon the Greeks. Six of each ship's company are struck down before Ulysses' men, taken by surprise, succeed in escaping. When they put out to sea, the ships are caught in a raging hurricane which drives them off their course. Their sails are ripped to pieces before they finally reach a sheltering coast. There the seafarers rest for two days. Then they sail on, but again contrary winds drive the ships off course.

"Thereafter for nine days I was driven
by ravening winds across the sea.
On the tenth day we made the land of the Lotos-eaters,
men who browse on a food of flowers . . .
as each tasted of this honey-sweet plant,
the wish to bring news or return grew faint in him:
rather he preferred to dwell for ever with the Lotos-eating men,
feeding upon Lotos and letting fade from his mind all memory of home.
I had to seek them and drag them back on board.
They wept: yet into the ships we brought them perforce and chained them
beneath the thwarts, deep in the well, while I constrained the rest
of my adherents to hurry aboard, lest perhaps more of them might eat
Lotos and lose their longing for home. They embarked promptly and
sat to the rowing benches; then in their proper ranks, all together,
they swung their oars and beat the sea hoary-white." (IX, 82–84, 94–104)

IN THE LAND OF THE CYCLOPES

As they sail on, Ulysses' fleet reaches the land of the Cyclopes. It is a very fertile land, bearing wheat, barley and noble vines. But the inhabitants, who are cruel giants, are not concerned with the crops. They live in caves in the rock of the mountains, each of them indifferent to the others. At the mouth of the bay formed by the land of the Cyclopes, toward which the twelve ships of

The pictures on the following pages show:

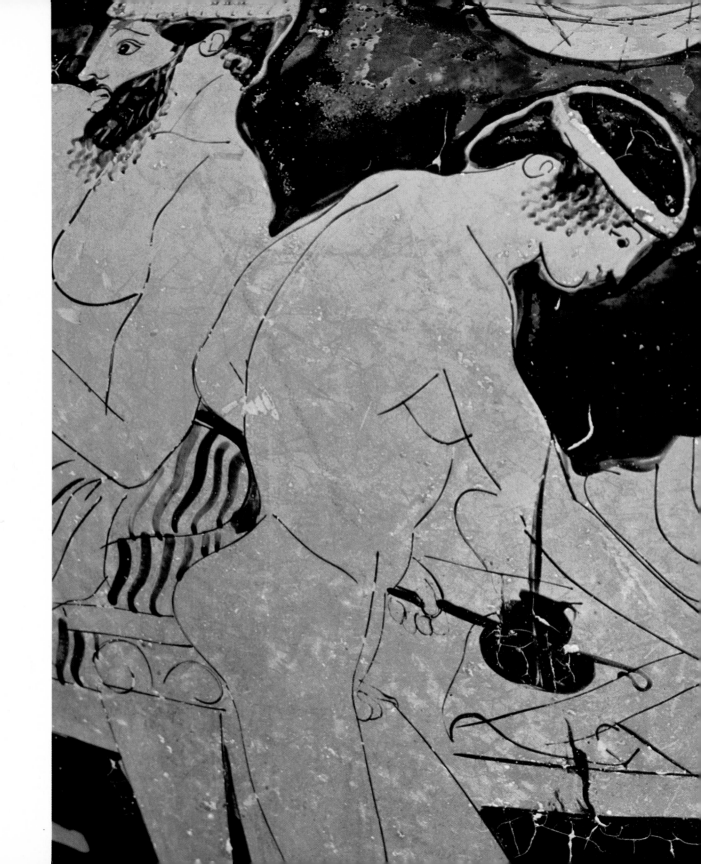

Ulysses steer, there is a little island inhabited only by goats. Here the seafarers find a natural harbor, protected from the winds, where they pass the night in safety. The next morning the crews take to hunting the wild goats. They take nine beasts for each ship and then have a festive meal on the uninhabited island. Early on the morning of the next day, Ulysses informs the assembled council of his ships that he intends to sail over in his ship to the land of the Cyclopes and explore the country.

"As we came to the nearest point of land
we could see a cave at its seaward extremity –
a lofty cave, embowered in laurels.
There were signs that large flocks of sheep and goats
were wont to be penned within it for the night.
Round the cave-mouth a strong-walled yard had been contrived of rocks
deeply embedded with a fence of logs from tall pines and spreading oaks.
Actually it was the lair of a giant,
a monstrous creature who pastured his flocks widely
from that centre and avoided traffic with any man.
He was a solitary infidel thing, this ogre, and fearfully made;
not in the fashion of a bread-eating man but altogether singular
and out-standing like a tree-grown crag of the high mountains." (IX, 181–192)

With twelve of his most courageous companions Ulysses disembarks to explore the cave. Along with provisions, the resourceful traveler takes with him a wineskin full of intoxicating, magical wine, a present which he had once been given by a priest of Apollo. For he suspected that in the course of his exploration he might have to use it against a man of monstrous strength.

Ulysses finds the cave empty. The Cyclops has taken his herds to pasture. Instead, the men find in the cave baskets of cheese and pails of milk. Ulysses' companions then propose to take as much of the provisions as they can carry and be off at once. But Ulysses is anxious to see the inhabitant of the cave, and persuades his companions to remain. So they eat a meal and then wait for the monster in the cave.

As evening is coming on, the Cyclops brings home his herds and thumps his way into the cave with a fearful din. The Greeks fly in terror to the farthest corner and watch with horror while the giant, using a stone which twenty-two four-wheeled wagons could not have stirred, stops the entrance of the cave. They are trapped. The fierce giant then tends his flocks, milks the sheep and the goats, and kindles a fire. The light of the flames reveals the Greeks, and the giant, in a voice of thunder, demands their names, where they come from and where they go.

The hoarse bellow of the giant leaves them all speechless with fright. But finally Ulysses summons up his strength and answers. He tells the giant that they are Greeks, on their way home from Troy, who have been driven off their course by storms. Then he asks for protection and welcome, in the name of the gods and the sacred rights of hospitality.

"Thus far I got: but the reply came from his pitiless heart.
'Sir Stranger, you are either very simple or very outlandish
if you bid me fear the gods and avoid crossing them. We are the Cyclopes

and being so much the bigger we listen not at all
to aegis-bearing Zeus or any blessed god.'"
                                        (IX, 272–276)

The Cyclops then asks where the Greeks have landed with their ships. But the wily Ulysses sees the danger of the question and answers in carefully pondered words: "Ah, my ship has been dashed to pieces on the reefs by Poseidon, shaker of the earth. Only these twelve companions and myself have escaped the awful doom."

"His savagery disdained me one word in reply.
He leapt to his feet, lunged with his hands among my fellows,
snatched up two of them like whelps and rapped their heads
against the ground. The brains burst out from their skulls
and were spattered over the cave's floor, while he broke them up,
limb from limb, and supped off them to the last shred,
eating ravenously like a mountain lion, everything –
bowels and flesh and bones, even to the marrow in the bones.
We wept and raised our hands to Zeus in horror at this crime
committed before our eyes; yet there was nothing we could do." (IX, 287–295)

When the Cyclops falls into a deep sleep after this cannibal meal, Ulysses first thinks to run him through with his sword. But then he recognizes that this offers no escape to himself and his companions, since they cannot possibly roll the mighty stone away from the entrance of the cave. The Greeks fall asleep, full of foreboding.

The next morning the Cyclops tends his herd, seizes for breakfast two more of the luckless Greeks, devours them and then leaves the cave with his beasts, closing the entrance again with the block of stone. The Greeks remain there, terror-stricken and trembling, each of them afraid that he will be the next to be slaughtered by the giant for his gruesome meal.

But Ulysses ponders a way of escape. From the giant's enormous club of green olivewood, as big as a ship's mast, he cuts a stake which will be a load for five men. He sets his companions to smooth it, while he himself gives it a sharp point which he hardens in the fire. Finally the resourceful hero hides the stake under the dung in the cave. Then he draws lots to choose the four companions who are to help him to thrust the stake into the monster's eye as soon as he is asleep.

When the giant returns in the evening, he again drives all the beasts into the cave, this time also bringing in the rams. He tends his flock and then devours for supper two more of Ulysses' companions. And now Ulysses starts to put his bold plan into action. He goes to the monster and offers him a beaker of the magically potent wine, saying:

"Cyclops, come now and on top of your meal of man's flesh
try this wine, to see how tasty a drink was hidden in our ship.
I brought it for you, hoping you would have compassion on me
and help me homeward: but your unwisdom is beyond all comprehending."
                                        (IX, 347–350)

The Cyclops swallows the drink and finds it excellent. Then he asks once more the name of Ulysses. But Ulysses first gives him three more beakers of wine and waits cautiously till the brain of the monster is fuddled by the drink. Then the resourceful Ulysses answers the Cyclops with sly words, saying:

"'Cyclops, you ask me for my public name: I will confess it to you aloud,
and do you then give me my guest-gift, as you have promised.
My name is No-man: so they have always called me, my mother and father
and all my friends.' I spoke, and he answered from his cruel heart,
'I will eat No-man finally, after all his friends. The others first –
that shall be your benefit.' He sprawled full-length, belly up,
on the ground, lolling his fat neck aside; and sleep that conquers all men
conquered him. Heavily he vomited out all his load of drink, and gobbets
of human flesh swimming in wine spurted gurgling from his throat." (IX, 364–374)

Then Ulysses and his surviving companions brace themselves for the second part of the well-devised plan of escape. They thrust the stake which they have prepared into the glowing embers and twist it till the point is glowing fiercely. Then they pull out the stake from the fire, and a god breathes courage into their souls:

"Some power from on high breathed into us all a mad courage,
by whose strength they charged with the great spear and stabbed
its sharp point right into his eye. I flung my weight upon it from above
so that it bored home. As a ship-builder's bit drills its timbers . . .
so we held the burning pointed stake in his eye and spun it,
till the boiling blood bubbled around its pillar of fire.
Eyebrows with eyelids shrivelled and stank in the blast
of his consuming eyeball . . . his eye sizzled about the olive-spike.
He let out a wild howl which rang round the cavern's walls."
                              (IX, 382–385, 388, 390, 395, 396)

The Greeks fly from the bellowing monster to take refuge in the utmost recesses of the cave. The blinded Cyclops snatches the stake from his eye, hurls it away from him and continues to roar, maddened with pain. His roars bring his brother Cyclopes hurrying from the neighboring caves. They stand before the cave and shout to Polyphemus, asking him what has happened and why he is shouting.

"Big Polyphemus yelled back to them from within his cave,
'My friends, No-man is killing me by sleight. There is no force about it.'
Wherefore they retorted cuttingly, 'If you are alone
and no one assaults you, but your pain is some unavoidable malady from Zeus,
why then, make appeal to your father King Poseidon.'
    They turned away and my dear heart laughed because the excellent
cunning trick of that false name had completely taken them in." (IX, 407–414)

But Polyphemus, the blinded giant, thinks bitterly of revenge. Groping his way to the opening of the cave, he feels for the block of stone and rolls it aside. Then he sits down at the entrance, groping around with his hands all the time, to catch any of the Greeks who may try to escape. Ulysses now braces himself for the third part of his plan of evasion. After pondering a long time, the best stratagem seems to be as follows:

"Some rams there were of big stock, fleecy great splendid beasts
with wool almost purple in its depth of colour.
I took them by threes silently and bound them abreast
with the pliant bark-strips from which the wicked monster's bed was plaited.
The middle beast could then take a man and the one
on either side protect him from discovery.
That meant three rams for each shipmate: while for myself
there remained the prize ram of all the flock. I took hold of him,
tucked myself under his shaggy belly and hung there so,
with steadfast courage: clinging face upwards
with my hands twisted into his enormous fleece.
Thus we waited in great trepidation for the dawn."
(IX, 425–436)

As the hungry beasts thrust their way out to pasture in the morning, the giant runs his fingers over their backs, but fails to touch any of the Greeks hidden under the beasts. And so the escape is successful. Outside the cave, the resourceful Ulysses frees his companions, and then they quickly drive the flock to the shore, where they load the beasts onto the ship and row out to sea.

But when the ship is as far from land as a voice will carry, Ulysses rises to his feet and mocks the blinded giant with insulting words. The giant bellows angrily, seizes a huge block of stone and casts it far into the sea. It almost hits the fleeing ship, and the wave thrown up as the missile smashes into the sea threatens to drive the craft back onto the shore. Ulysses has to use a great pole to push the ship off the strand, and the Greeks row fast out to sea again. Once more, though this time from twice as far out, Ulysses calls to the raging giant. He jeers at him, in spite of his companions' pleas for silence, because the Cyclops' great throw has missed the ship. And then he cries out:

"'If any human being asks of you how your eye was so hideously put out,
say that Ulysses, despoiler of cities, did it;
even the son of Laertes, whose home is in Ithaca.' Thus I shouted . . .
But he lifted up his hands to the starry firmament and prayed to
his Lord, Poseidon. 'Hear me, dark-haired Girdler of the earth,
if indeed I am yours and you my sire. Grant that there be no
home-coming for this Ulysses, son of Laertes of Ithaca.
Yet if it is fated that he must see his friends once more
in his stately house and fatherland, let it be late
and miserably, in a strange ship, after losing all his crews.

The pictures on the following pages show:

And let him find trouble there in the house.' So he made his petition
and the dark god heard him. Then the giant bent to another stone
(much larger than before), whirled it with immeasurable force and let it fly."

(IX, 502–505, 526–538)

But the rock again misses the ship, and Ulysses rejoins the rest of his fleet at the Isle of Goats
without mishap. On the shore, he offers sacrifice to Zeus, the gatherer of the clouds, but Zeus
disdains the sacrifice. So it is with heavy hearts that Ulysses and his companions hoist sail the
next morning.

AEOLUS' FLASK

AND THE BATTLE WITH THE LAESTRYGONIANS

Sailing onward, Ulysses' fleet comes to the island of Aeolus, the god of the winds. The hero
stays as Aeolus' guest for a month on the island, which is surrounded by a gleaming wall of bronze
and smooth-faced stone, telling the lord of the island of the battles for Troy. When saying farewell, the lord of the winds gives Ulysses the divine a wineskin, staunch and tightly stoppered,
in which all contrary winds have been bottled away. And he sends the hero a gentle west wind
to carry him happily on his homeward journey. Borne on by the favorable wind, the ships sail
homeward for nine days and nine nights. On the tenth night they can already recognize the
beacons of their island home, Ithaca. And Ulysses, who has himself been standing at the rudder
all this time, lies down to sleep, feeling that his home-coming is now certain.

But Ulysses' companions, imagining that the flask given by the wind-god Aeolus is filled
with priceless treasures, are plagued by envy. They decide to open the flask. The captive winds
rush out, whip the waves into a mighty storm, and drive the ships back to the island of Aeolus.
Ulysses tries to secure once more the aid of the lord of the winds, but Aeolus answers:

"'Get off the island instantly, you vilest thing alive!
Am I to make a habit of maintaining and fitting out
one whom the gods hate? Your being returned proves that you have incurred
the abhorrence of those Deathless Ones. Out! out!'
His words drove me from the house in grief. Our sailing was gloomy:
and now we had no helping wind, wherefore we must labour continually
at the oars, by which futile pain my men's fortitude was sapped." (X, 67–74)

After a voyage of six days and nights the fleet reaches the land of the Laestrygonians. The
ships sail into the bay which serves as a sheltering harbour, surrounded by steep rocky cliffs,
and cast anchor near the shore. Ulysses alone anchors his ship at the mouth of the bay. Then
he sends a herald with two companions to explore. They succeed in making their way to the
citadel of the Laestrygonian king, Antiphates. But here a gruesome fate awaits them. The king
seizes one of the Greeks and dishes him up for food.

"The other two sprang away in headlong flight
and regained the ships, while the master of the house
was sounding an alarm through the city.
This brought the stout Laestrygonians in their thousands
pell-mell together – not human-looking creatures, these, but giants.
They gathered missile stones each a man's weight and cast them
down on us off the cliffs. There went up from the fleet
the ghastly sounds of splintering hulls and dying men,
while the natives were busy spearing my people like fish
and collecting them to make their loathsome meal." (X, 117–124)

Ulysses' fleet is destroyed, and his men fall victim to the monstrous cannibals. Only Ulysses himself, who had been moved by a cautious surmise to anchor his ship at a distance from the cliffs, has time to hew away the anchorlines with his sword, and escape with his crew by standing out to sea.

"So it was in very disheartened mood that we rowed on,
having lost every one of our dear comrades
(yet with the consolation that we were still alive) . . ." (X, 133–134)

With these words Ulysses gives the account of his adventures to the astonished listeners at the court of the king of the Phaeacians, Alcinous.

THE SORCERESS CIRCE

Soon after escaping from the attack of the man-eating Laestrygonians, Ulysses' ship is bearing down on the island of Aeaea. This was the dwelling place of the goddess Circe, whose mother was the daughter of Oceanus. Ulysses steers his ship into a sheltering bay, where the Greeks rest for two full days, worn out by their desperate struggle. On the morning of the third day, Ulysses sets out to explore the land. Wary and on the alert, he moves about the strange island and when he sees smoke rising in the distance, returns to the ship, fearing to fall alone into some trap.

On his way back, he succeeds in killing a deer, which means that his crew can again at last enjoy fresh meat.

On the morning of the next day Ulysses tells his companions of what he has seen on the island. His men are timid and hesitant, remembering the terrible experiences which lie behind them. But Ulysses insists that the place from which he saw the smoke rising should be surveyed by a large number of men. He divides his crew into two groups, one half led by himself, the other under Eurylochus. Then they draw lots to decide which party is to move out. The lot points to Eurylochus, and he sets forth with twenty-two companions. The party reaches the palace of the goddess, and they find themselves fawned on by lions and wolves. These, though the Greeks do not know it, are men transformed by the goddess's spells. Hearing their cries, the goddess herself appears.

She came at once, opening her doors to bid them in.
In their simplicity all went in to her: all except Eurylochus
who suspected some trick und stayed behind.
She showed them all to thrones and seats and confected for them
a mess of cheese with barley-meal and clear honey, mulched in Pramnian wine.
With this she mixed drugs so sadly powerful
as to steal from them all memory of their native land.
After they had drunk from the cup she struck them with her wand;
and straightway hustled them to her sties,
for they grew the heads and shapes and bristles of a swine,
with swine-voices too. Only their reason remained steadfastly as before . . . (X, 230–240)

Eurylochus brings the new tale of woe and terror to Ulysses and his companions. Trembling with fear, Eurylochus refuses to show Ulysses the way to the goddess's palace. So the hero sets out alone. On the way, not far from the palace of the dreadful sorceress, he is met by Hermes, the messenger of the gods. He confirms that Circe has used her magical spells to turn the Greeks into swine and warns Ulysses of his danger. Then he gives him a magical plant which protects him against the goddess's potions and tells him how he can gain the upper hand and free his companions from the goddess's power.

Protected by the magical plant, Ulysses consumes unharmed the drink which the lovely, treacherous goddess offers him in token of welcome. For when the goddess, having seen the potion drunk, touches Ulysses with her magic wand to turn him into a pig like his companions, the divine hero remains impervious to the spell. And then Ulysses puts into execution the advice of Hermes, messenger of the gods:

"I drew sword sharply and leapt up, feigning to make an end of her.
She gave a shrill scream, ran in under my stroke and clasped
my knees in a flood of tears, while she wailed piercingly,
'What kind of man are you; from what city or family?
It is a miracle how you have drunk my potion and not been bewitched.
Never before, never, has any man resisted this drug, once it
passed his lips and crossed the barrier of his jaws.
How firmly seated must be your indomitable mind!
Surely you are Ulysses the resourceful, who will come here
(as Argusbane of the golden rod often tells me)
on his way from Troy in his ship.'" (X, 321–332)

Shrinking from Ulysses' threats and seeing no escape, the sorceress now swears that he shall come to no harm. She gives him hospitality as her guest, and the favors of her love. But Ulysses thinks first of his bewitched companions, and the terrible goddess finally undoes the spell by smearing the backs of the bristling swine with a healing ointment. His companions, now younger and handsomer than before, cluster round Ulysses weeping tears of joy. Even the sorceress is moved, and she invites Ulysses to fetch his other companions from the ship and to moor it securely to the shore, so that all can join in a festive meal.

Ulysses yields to the goddess, who bestows such lavish hospitality that the whole company are ready to stay on in her palace, with hardly a thought of the passage of time or of their journey home.

"We tarried day by day till an entire year had lapsed,
sitting to table and delighting in her untold wealth of flesh
and mellow wine. Slowly the year fulfilled itself,
as the seasons turned about and the months died,
bringing down the long days once more. Then my men took me aside, saying:
'Master, it is time you called to memory your native land,
if fate will ever let you come alive to your well-built house
and ancient estate.' So they said, and my nobility assented to them."

(X, 467–475)

The following night the godlike Ulysses, fated to be sorely tried, demands imperiously of the love-stricken goddess that she should finally speed him and his companions on their homeward journey, as she has promised. The goddess yields, but then reveals to the terrified hero that he must first journey to Hades, to offer sacrifice there in the Underworld and to ask the seer Teiresias what ways and means will bring him safely home through the deeps.

The next morning Ulysses goes and wakens his companions from sleep, to tell them of the goddess's dire tidings. Reluctant and lamenting, the Greeks then make ready to sail and set out on their journey to the end of the ocean, where the entrance to the Underworld lies, not far from the land of the Cimmerians, men who spend their lives groping in gloomy fogs, under the dark shadow of a sinister night.

IN THE UNDERWORLD

Arriving at the entrance of the Underworld, the Greeks offer sacrifice, as the goddess Circe has advised them. The resourceful Ulysses uses his sword to cut the throats of the victims, letting the dark blood flow down the pitted earth, so that the souls of the dead, in their thirst for the blood, will come up from the Underworld, the kingdom of Hades and Persephone.

"I took the two sheep and beheaded them across my pit
in such manner that the livid blood drained into it.
Then from out of Erebus they flocked to me,
the dead spirits of those who had died.
Brides came and lads; old men and men of sad experience;
tender girls aching from their first agony;
and many fighting men showing the stabbed wounds of brazen spears –
war-victims still in their blooded arms. All thronged to the trench
and raged restlessly this side of it and that with an eerie wailing.
Pale fear gripped me . . .

I sat over the pit holding out my sharp weapon to forbid
and prevent this shambling legion of the dead from approaching
the blood till I had had my answer from Teiresias." (XI, 36–43, 48–50)

The noble-hearted Ulysses must prevent even the soul of his mother from approaching the pit. He sheathes his sword only when the figure of the aged seer of Thebes, Teiresias, appears, and lets him drink of the dark blood. The inspired seer then reveals the future to Ulysses. First, Teiresias says, the hero's wanderings will bring him to the island of Thrinacia, where the Oxen of the Sun have their pastures. If the Greeks leave the sacred beasts unharmed, they will surely have a quick passage home. But if they kill any of the beasts, the ship and its crew are doomed to destruction. Only Ulysses will reach home again, after many tribulations and long delays. And Ulysses is fated to further wanderings, the seer predicts, which will take him to men who do not know the sea and mistake a rudder for a shovel, after he has driven the arrogant suitors from his palace. There he must offer sacrifice to Poseidon, whose wrath is still unabated, and to the other gods. Then death will overtake him only at a great age, serene among comforts.

Having thus foretold the destiny of the godlike Ulysses, the aged Teiresias returns to the world of the shadows. And now the other souls throng to the pit, led by the mother of the sorely tried hero. He lets them drink and questions them all, these wraiths from the past. The soul of the luckless Agamemnon also appears. Ulysses sees Achilles and his friend Patroclus, and then the figure of the terrible Ajax. Even the godlike Heracles appears, and the figure of the luckless Sisyphus. But in the end Ulysses is stricken by horror and dread at this monstrous stream of specters, and he hastens back to his ship with his companions. There they set sail, from the end of the ocean, to return to the sheltering island of the sorceress Circe.

THE SIRENS, SCYLLA AND CHARYBDIS

The Greeks rest for a night on the shore of the island. In the morning, the goddess appears with her maidservants and brings them food and drink.

"She stood in our midst, saying:
'A hardy adventure, men, this going down to Hades alive.
Now you will twice encounter death, whereas others do die but once.
So I pray you rest here on the island all today, eating my food
and drinking this wine. If you sail tomorrow at the daybreak
I shall have time to plot you a course and detail its leading-marks:
that you may be saved the hurt and pain of untoward,
unforeseen accidents by sea or land.'" (XII, 20–27)

And the goddess warns Ulysses of the further hazards that are to be encountered. She gives him wise counsel, to help him to escape the danger of the bewitching Sirens, and to come safely through the passage between the terrors of Scylla and Charybdis. She then bids farewell to the resourceful Ulysses, and speeds them on their way with a favorable wind. The Greeks soon reach the open sea.

There Ulysses tells his companions of the dangers disclosed by Circe, and repeats her advice. And when they draw near to the islands of the Sirens, he stops his companions' ears with wax, so that they may not be bewitched by the magical songs of the Sirens and throw themselves into the sea to perish miserably. He leaves his own ears unstopped, but has himself bound to the mast, warning his companions not to set him free, no matter how urgent his entreaties, but only to bind him more strongly.

"Then they tied me stiffly upright to the tabernacle,
with extra ends of rope made fast to the mast above.
Once more they sat and their oar-beats whitened the sea.
Speeding thus lightly we arrived within earshot of the place.
The Sirens became aware of the sea-swift vessel running by them:
wherefore they clearly sang to us their song – 'Hither, come
hither, O much-praised Ulysses: come to us, O Glory of Achaea.
Bring your ship to land that you may listen to our twin voices.
Never yet has any man in a dark ship passed us by
without lending ear to the honey-sweet music of our lips –
to go away spirit-gladdened and riper in knowledge.
For we know all the toils wherewith the gods did afflict
Argives and Trojans in the broad Troad: and we know all things
which shall be hereafter upon the fecund earth.'
Such words they sang in lovely cadences. My heart ached to hear them out.
To make the fellows loose me I frowned upon them with my brows.
They bent to it ever the more stoutly while Perimedes and Eurylochus
rose to tighten my former bonds and wreathed me about and about
with new ones: and so it was till we were wholly past them
and could no more hear the Sirens' words nor their tune." (XII, 178–198)

Ulysses' ship has barely escaped the danger of the Sirens' charms when the terrified Greeks hear in the distance the dull thud of the breakers and the hollow roar that rises from the swirling waters of Charybdis. Ulysses urges his companions to row on boldly, and advises the helmsman to steer close to the rock, so that the ship may not be caught by the raging whirlpool of Charybdis and sucked down into the gloomy depths. But the wise Ulysses does not speak of Scylla to his companions, who are already almost paralyzed by fear, so as not to increase their anxiety. For the goddess Circe, the enchantress, had described the monster Scylla to the hero:

"She has twelve splay feet and six lank scrawny necks.
Each neck bears an obscene head, toothy with three rows
of thick-set crowded fangs blackly charged with death.
She keeps herself bedded waist-deep in the bowels of her cave
but sways her heads out across the dizzy void . . .
never failing to snatch up a man with each one of her heads
from every dark-prowed ship that comes. No sailors yet can boast
to have slipped past her in their craft, scot-free." (XII, 89–94, 98–100)

So the Greeks, not knowing the twofold danger that threatens them, row boldly toward the rocky channel, while the helmsman is careful to steer clear of all the swirling eddies at which the rowers gaze in terror.

"My crew turned sallow with fright, staring into this abyss
from which we expected our immediate death.
Scylla chose the moment to rape from the midst of the ship
six of our party – the six stoutest and best.
I happened to cast my eye back along the thwarts, over the crew,
and thus marked their dangling hands and feet as they
were wrenched aloft, screeching my name for the last time
in voices made thin and high by agony . . .
So did they swing writhing upward to the cliffs;
where in her cave-mouth she chewed and swallowed them,
despite their screaming and stretching of hands in final appeal
to me for help in their death agony. This was the most
pitiful thing of all the sorrows that ever my eyes did see
while I explored the by-ways of the deep."

(XII, 244–250, 255–259)

But the ship carries the rest of the company safely through the deadly straits and reaches the island of Thrinacia, where they already hear in the distance the Oxen of the Sun and his sacred sheep, bellowing and bleating.

THE ATTACK ON THE SACRED OXEN

On sighting the island, Ulysses remembers the prophecy of Teiresias and the warnings of Circe, that this island could mean terrible calamity for himself and his companions, through their own fault. He advises his companions to avoid the island and sail on at once. But his loyal comrades, who have survived so many dangers together, refuse to steer for the high seas after the terrors which they have just experienced from Scylla and Charybdis. They wish to spend at least one night on solid ground, to eat and drink and recover their strength. So Ulysses warns them once more not to lay hands on the sacred beasts, and with a heavy heart commands the ship to head for the land.

But during the night, Zeus, the gatherer of the clouds, sends a tempest which forces the sailors to haul the ship completely ashore. For a whole month, Ulysses' men are detained on the island by contrary winds. With Ulysses' warning ringing in their ears, they observe for a while the ban on killing the sacred beasts, and nourish themselves from their dwindling provisions. But one day Ulysses, disturbed by the threat of famine, goes out alone to beg counsel of the gods for his homeward journey. The gods send him a deep and refreshing sleep, and while he is absent, Eurylochus instigates his companions to act:

47

"'No variety of death is pleasing to us poor mortals: but commend
me to hunger and its slow perishing as the meanest fate of all.
Up therefore; let us take our pick of the Sun's cattle
and dedicate them in death to all the gods of heaven.
If ever we do reach Ithaca, our own, there can we quickly erect
some splendid fane for Helios Hyperion and fill it with every precious gift.
But if he is angered enough by the loss of his high-horned cattle
to want the ruin of our ship, and if the other gods cry yea to him –
why then, I choose to quit life with one gulp in the sea
rather than waste to death here by inches in this desert island.'
So said Eurylochus and the rest agreed.
The cattle of the Sun were then to hand . . .
Forthwith the fellows drove aside the choicest . . ." (XII, 341–353)

When Ulysses wakes from his sleep and returns to the strand, he sees with horror the monstrous crime of his companions. And meanwhile, the news of the slaughter of his sacred beasts has also reached Helios, the sun-god. He complains bitterly to Zeus and the other gods on Mount Olympus, threatening that he will withhold his light from the earth if he is not avenged and paid satisfaction.

"Zeus answered him and said: 'Nay, Helios: do you go on shining amongst the gods
and for the mortals who go their ways about the fertile earth.
Upon me be it to smite their ship with one cast of my white thunderbolt
and shiver it amid the wine-dark sea.'" (XII, 384–388)

In vain Ulysses berates his companions. He cannot undo the crime. And gloomy presages at once begin to appear. The skins of the slaughtered oxen start to creep around, and the meat on the roasting-spits as well as the uncooked parts start to emit bellows like living oxen. But this does not prevent the company from feasting for six whole days on the gains of their crime.

When the storm finally drops on the seventh day, the Greeks embark and put out to sea for the homeward journey. But scarcely has the island sunk beneath the horizon when the dreadful revenge of Zeus falls upon the ship and its unhappy crew. The two masts snap in a whirlwind, and as they crash to the deck they kill the helmsman. Then bolts of lightning strike the ship as it is driven wildly to and fro by the raging waves, killing all who ate of the sacred oxen. The flashing lightning hurled by the angry Father of the gods spares only Ulysses, who succeeds, as the ship breaks up under the crashing waves, in getting a line around the drifting keel and the masthead and tying them together as a makeshift raft. Climbing aboard, he rides out the storm for the night. But in the morning, the wind changes and drives him into the whirlpool of dreadful Charybdis, into which the raft disappears. Ulysses saves himself by clinging to the branch of a fig-tree which overhangs the rock. There he remains hour after hour, suspended over the raging whirlpool, till his raft of keel and masthead bobs up once more from the eddies. Then, with the courage of despair, the hero lets himself fall into the water, straddles the beams, and succeeds at last, paddling with his hands, in escaping from the whirlpool and then from the menace of Scylla.

48

The pictures on the following pages show:

"So I drifted for nine days. In the tenth darkness the gods cast me
ashore on Ogygia, where lives Calypso the high but humane-spoken goddess
who greeted me kindly and tended me. Yet why rehearse all that?
Only yesterday I told it within to you, O King, and to your famous wife.
It goes against my grain to repeat a tale already plainly told." (XII, 447–453)

With these words the sorely tried Ulysses ends the story of his home-coming, while King Alcinous and the Phaeacians listen in stunned silence to his adventures.

THE HOME-COMING OF ULYSSES

Deeply moved by the story of the godlike Ulysses, King Alcinous orders that his princes should each add a great tripod to their gifts, and fixes the following day for the voyage home. Still another banqet is prepared in honor of the princely guest, then Ulysses says farewell and boards the waiting vessel, into which the Phaeacians have loaded their parting gifts.

"The crew took station along their thwarts.
They cast off the cable from its ring-stone and bent to their work,
spuming the sea high with their oarblades:
while a sleep that was flawless closed down upon the eyes of Ulysses –
a most sweet sleep, profound, and in semblance very near to death." (XIII, 78–80)

By the early dawn the Phaeacian oarsmen, famous throughout the Mediterranean for their speed and endurance, have reached the island of Ithaca. They moor their ship in a bay sacred to the sea-god Phorcys, not far from the city.

They filed down off her benches,
raised Ulysses from the hollow hull and bore him to land
just as he was, on his sheet and gay carpet.
He was yet lost in sleep as they bedded him gently on the sand.
Then they passed ashore his belongings, the treasures with which
by Athene's contriving the Phaeacian nobles had speeded his parting.
These they piled in a little heap against the olive-trunk,
aside from the road for fear some wayfarer might pass
while Ulysses still slept; and plunder him.
Then they pushed off for home. (XIII 116–125)

But Poseidon, the lord of the seas, looks with grim disfavor on this home-coming of Ulysses. Burning with anger, he appears before the assembly of the gods and demands of Zeus, now that Ulysses has escaped him, that he may at least be avenged on the rescuers of the resourceful Ulysses, the ship and oarsmen of the Phaeacians. This Zeus grants him, to placate the wrath of the god. Poseidon betakes himself swiftly to the city of the Phaeacians, to await the return of

49

the speedy oarsmen. When the ship has almost reached the shore, the god of the sea strikes it with the flat of his hand and turns it into stone in mid-course. The Phaeacians watching from the shore are terror-stricken at the vengeance of the sea-god and make haste, at Alcinous' orders, to offer a sacrifice to Poseidon on the seashore, to placate the angry god and forestall further punishments.

But at this moment, in Ithaca, the godlike Ulysses is waking from a refreshing sleep. Athene, however, the bountiful goddess, has changed all the countryside around him so completely that Ulysses no longer recognizes it.

He rose to his feet and stood staring at what was his own land,
then sighed and clapped his two palms downward upon his thighs,
crying mournfully, "Alas! and now where on earth am I?" (XIII, 197–200)

Filled with despair, Ulysses believes at this moment that the Phaeacians have abandoned him on a foreign strand, while also robbing him of his gifts, the tokens of their hospitality. But then he recognizes the gifts, which have been piled into a heap, and when he counts them, they are all there. This brings him a moment's consolation, but then he is again overcome by sadness at the thought of his lost homeland, and he wanders about the seashore, in tears.

There he is met by his protectress, the goddess Athene, now in the guise of a handsome young shepherd. Ulysses is cheered by the sight of the figure, and hastens to greet the young man, asking him what country he is in. And the goddess describes the island in terms of high praise and then gives its name. It is Ithaca.

Her word made great Ulysses' heart leap for happiness
in this his native land, now divine Athene made him aware of it.
To her he again uttered winged words; yet not true words,
for he swallowed back what had been on his lips
to make play with the very cunning nature instinctive in him. (XIII, 250–254)

And so the resourceful Ulysses, who has not recognized the goddess in the form of the young shepherd, spins a long tale of battles and adventures which have cast him up on this island, without giving his name.

As he was running on the goddess broke into a smile
and petted him with her hand. She waxed tall: she turned womanly:
she was beauty's mistress, dowered with every accomplishment of taste.
Then she spoke to him in words which thrilled:
"Any man, or even any god, who would keep pace
with your all-round craftiness must needs be a canny dealer and sharp-practised.
O plausible, various, cozening wretch, can you not even in your native place
let be these crooked and shifty words which so delight the recesses of your mind?
Enough of such speaking in character between us two past-masters
of these tricks of trade – you, the cunningest mortal
to wheedle or blandish, and me, famed above other gods for knavish wiles.

And yet you failed to recognize in me the daughter of Zeus,
Pallas Athene, your stand-by and protection throughout your toils!
It was thanks to me that you were welcomed by the entire society of the Phaeacians . . ."
(XIII, 287–302)

Still Ulysses does not dare to believe beyond doubt that he has come home to Ithaca. But Athene lets him see the place where he is standing, and gives the name of the bay and of the Cave of the Nymphs nearby and the towering Mount Neriton. And then she dissipates the cloud which has made everything seem strange to Ulysses' eyes.

The joy of seeing his own place so wrought upon Ulysses
that he fell to kissing its bounteous soil . . . (XIII, 351–352)

Then the hero and the goddess hide the treasures of the Phaeacians safely in the sacred Cave of the Nymphs and then discuss the surest way of putting the suitors to death. Athene promises Ulysses her help. She will first transform him into the guise of an old beggarman, so that none of the suitors will recognize the returned wanderer. The goddess then charges the hero as follows:

"You will begin by joining company with the swineherd
who keeps your swine: a man of single heart toward yourself
and devoted to your son and judicious Penelope.
You will find him watching his beasts
grubbing round the Raven's Crag and Arethusa's fountain.
Thereby they grow into fat and healthy pigs, by virtue
of the acorns they love and the still waters of the spring they drink.
Sit with him and wait, learning all his news
till I have been to Sparta, the land of fair women, and recalled
your dear son Telemachus
who went to the house of Menelaus, there in wide Lacedaemon,
trying to find out if you are still alive." (XIII, 402–413)

Then the daughter of Zeus transforms the hero into the guise of a ragged old beggarman with sunken eyes, and the two set off together.

ULYSSES AND THE SWINEHERD EUMAEUS

Ulysses leaves the harbour and climbs the hill to the pastures of the swineherd Eumaeus, whom he knows to be his most loyal servant. There on the plateau there are twelve sties where the herdsman with his helpers tends six hundred sows, and as well as these, the boars which are fattened for the table of the arrogant suitors. The herds are guarded by four ravenous wolfhounds. When the hounds see the beggarman approaching, they hurl themselves upon him, ready to tear him in pieces. But the wise Ulysses quickly lays aside his staff and sits down on the ground, until the

51

swineherd Eumaeus calls off the hounds and invites the wanderer to his hut, to give him food and drink.

During the meal, for which Eumaeus roasted two suckling pigs for the beggarman, the loyal servant laments repeatedly the fate of his master, stranded in some foreign land, and the base conduct of the suitors. But Ulysses does not make himself known. When the swineherd asks him his name and where he comes from and whither he goes, Ulysses responds, as he had done with Athene, by telling a story of strange adventures, mingling truth and fiction. He claims to be a Greek from Crete who has fought at Troy, with Ulysses. And as he tells his story he slips in again and again the hint that Ulysses is soon to return. But the herdsman, disappointed so often during the long years of waiting, cannot bring himself to believe in the return of his royal master Ulysses. Nonetheless, he gives the beggarman a princely welcome and prepares for him a soft bed of fleeces for the night.

Meanwhile, Athene has gone to Sparta, where Telemachus is still at the court. She tells him that he must now return to Ithaca, where the suitors are behaving more and more arrogantly and pressing harder and harder for a decision from his mother Penelope. And the goddess also warns Ulysses' son of the ambush set up by the murderous suitors.

When Telemachus is about to set out, accompanied by Peisistratus, the son of King Nestor, with rich gifts from Menelaus and Helen, a mighty eagle, coming from the right, suddenly flies over the chariot, clutching in his talons a fat white goose. All the spectators are convinced that this is an omen sent by the gods. Helen, the beautiful queen, interprets the sign:

"Hear me, while I declare the meaning (surely the true meaning)
which the gods have flashed into my mind.
As that eagle from the mountain eyrie which the eagles haunt
has borne off in one swoop our farm-fattened goose,
so shall Ulysses come back from his sore wandering and avenge himself:
unless perhaps he is already home and brooding ruin for the suitors." (XV, 171–177)

Encouraged by the good omen, the two princes travel swiftly to Pylos. There Telemachus embarks at once and heads his ship for home, to Ithaca. Under the protection of Athene, Telemachus succeeds in reaching a hidden, landlocked bay, evading the ambush of the bloodthirsty suitors. He then commands his men to row the ship into the port of the city. His own first step will be to arrange matters with his herdsman Eumaeus.

The men row off, and Telemachus sets out for Eumaeus' hut. He arrives there just as the herdsman and Ulysses are preparing the morning meal. When Eumaeus recognizes Telemachus, he lets the dishes drop from his hands, in a joy mingled with terror.

With tears of joy he met his lord, to kiss his head, his eyes, his hands,
as a good father greets the darling of his heart, his only and beloved son,
home after ten long anxious years. Just so the good swineherd clung to the prince
and embraced him like one snatched from death, while he cried out:
"Your coming, O Telemachus, is sweetness and light.
After you had sailed for Pylos I whispered to myself
that I had seen you for the last time.

Come in, my child, come in to the house,
that my heart may be gladdened by the wanderer's return." (XVI, 15–26)

When the beggarman, Ulysses, stands up to make place for Telemachus, the young prince begs him politely to remain seated. And Eumaeus hastily tells the prince that the stranger comes from Crete and has asked the swineherd for shelter. Telemachus too takes the stranger under his protection, but advises him to stay with the swineherd, since the palace is in disorder through the monstrous behavior of the suitors. Telemachus then asks Eumaeus to go quickly to the palace and tell his mother, the noble Penelope, of the happy return of her son.

When Athene sees that Ulysses is alone with his son in the hut, she appears in the form of a young girl, visible only to Ulysses. She beckons the resourceful traveler outside the hut, where she can speak to him alone, and then utters the winged words:

She said: "God-begotten, cease hiding from your son.
Open yourself to him and concert a way to slaughter the suitors.
Then start together for the famous town. Nor will I lag behind.
I am longing for the fray." She touched him with her golden rod
and clothed his body anew in laundered robes.
She restored his stature and presence. His flesh took on colour,
his cheeks filled out. The dark beard bushed once more about his chin. (XVI, 67–76)

The goddess vanishes, and Ulysses re-enters the hut. Telemachus, full of awe at the astonishing change in the stranger, takes him for a divine being and begs for grace, promising him rich sacrifices. Then the noble sufferer Ulysses answers him:

"I am no god: liken me not with the immortals.
In very deed I am your father, the Ulysses
for whose sake you have grieved and endured adversity
and suffered indignities from men." He spoke and kissed the lad,
yielding to the tears he had hitherto held back. (XVI, 86–91)

Telemachus scarcely dares to believe the joyful news, and continues to doubt whether the majestic stranger is really his father, home again. But Ulysses at last convinces him, and when they both have wept many tears of joy, they discuss the terrible fate which Ulysses is now ready to bring down upon the suitors, with the help of Athene and Zeus, the hurler of lightning. Telemachus, as his father now orders, is to return the next morning to the palace in the city. Ulysses is to follow him, in the guise of a beggarman. And he urges his son to be patient, no matter what indignities the suitors inflict on the miserable beggarman. Telemachus is to wait and watch, until Athene gives his father a sign, merely holding swords and spears in readiness for himself and his father when they set about their grim work of vengeance. But until this work is in hand, no one is to know of the return of Ulysses, neither the faithful Penelope nor the watchful Eumaeus. So the resourceful Ulysses impresses on his son. And then in the evening, as the swineherd returns from the city, Athene once more gives the godlike Ulysses the form of the ragged beggarman, under whose miserable figure no one can recognize the hero.

During this time, since the arrival of Telemachus' ship, the news of his happy return has spread rapidly throughout Ithaca. Raging with anger, the suitors recognize that their murderous plot has failed. When the suitors' ship returns, having waited in vain to set upon the king's son, Antinous, the boldest of them, declares: Even if it was a god who helped Telemachus to return safely, and even though he has escaped their ambush unseen, he must not find safety in the palace. Penelope, full of care, who has heard of the plot and now appears before the suitors, deeply disturbed, is reassured by them that no one thinks of murder. But in their dark hearts they have resolved on their crime and think of how to execute their new plan.

ULYSSES IN HIS PALACE

As had been decided the day before by the father and son, Telemachus hastens next day to the palace in the city, as soon as the sun is up. There his first thought is to tell his mother Penelope, after warm greetings, of his journey to Pylos and Sparta, and of what he there learned of the fortunes of Ulysses. Ulysses, in the guise of a beggarman, is also on his way to the city, in the company of the faithful swineherd Eumaeus. They meet on the way the goatherd Melanthius, who fails of course to recognize his master in the guise of a beggar, and thrusts him away with his foot, berating him. Ulysses bears the ill-treatment patiently, mindful of his disguise.

When Eumaeus and the beggarman reach the gates of the palace, Ulysses is recognized by his dog Argus, which Ulysses had himself trained to hunt many years ago. Feeble with age, the dog is lying on dung, neglected by all, since his master can no longer take care of him.

Yet the instant Ulysses approached, the beast knew him.
He thumped his tail and drooped his ears forward, but lacked power
to drag himself ever so little towards his master. However, Ulysses
saw him out of the corner of his eye and brushed away a tear . . . (XVII, 301–304)

Ulysses and Eumaeus now enter the banqueting hall, where the suitors are again gathered for a sumptuous meal. Ulysses sits down on the ground near the door, as befits a beggar. But Telemachus calls the swineherd over to him, gives him as much bread and meat as his hands will hold, and tells him to bring the food to the beggarman. And he also gives orders that the beggarman should be allowed to move freely around the table of the suitors. When the singer who has been performing during the suitors' meal has finished his song, Ulysses rises to his feet, urged on once more by Athene, and goes to the suitors' table to ask them for food. The suitors give him food, but the shepherd Melanthius, he who had already insulted the beggarman, now mocks him again, and with him his companion Eumaeus. His words provoke the malicious Antinous to hurl abuse at the swineherd and then at Ulysses, who has asked again for food. Raging angrily, he finally seizes a footstool, swings it at Ulysses and shouts:

"For your saucy speaking I shall make sure you do not get away
from the hall in good order"; and upon the word he swung
his footstool and hurled it to hit him on the right side,
just where the arm roots into the back.

54

Ulysses stood up against the blow like a rock; only he
wagged his head in silence, while a black rage swelled within him.

(XVII, 460–465)

The other suitors condemn Antinous' action, but Antinous belittles their compassion for the sufferer. In the women's quarters, Penelope has also heard of the arrival of the strange beggarman. She sends a message to Eumaeus to tell him:

"Good Eumaeus, bid the stranger come up to receive my hearty
greeting and be asked if he has heard anything of Ulysses,
or seen him, perchance; for he looks a much-travelled man." (XVII, 508–511)

Eumaeus conveys to the beggarman the wishes of the queen, and tells him that Penelope will give him a new tunic and robe to wear, if his story is true. But Ulysses, skilled in many wiles, tells Eumaeus that he would rather wait for nightfall to go to the queen, to avoid fresh insults from the suitors for visiting the queen in his rags. Penelope rests content with this answer. Toward evening a beggarman from Ithaca, called Irus, comes to the palace and tries to drive Ulysses from the threshold. When Ulysses tells him that there is surely room enough for the two beggarmen on the threshold of the palace, Irus answers him with scorn and challenges the older man to fisticuffs. The arrogant suitors find the beggarmen's quarrel amusing and try to urge on the contestants by promising that the victor in the battle of fists will have free choice among all the victuals. When the suitors then swear to the resourceful Ulysses that they will not punish him if he vanquishes the ill-mannered Irus, the hero makes ready to fight. When Irus sees the sinewy arms, the deep chest and broad shoulders of the supposed beggarman, he trembles with terror. But the suitors force him to prepare likewise for the fight.

Royal Ulysses was puzzling himself
if it were better to smite the other so starkly that life would leave him
where he fell, or to tap him gently and just stretch him out.
On the whole the gentle way seemed right, to save himself
from too close notice by the Achaeans. So when they put up their hands
and Irus hit at his right shoulder Ulysses only hooked him to the neck
under the ear and crushed the bones inward, so that blood
gushed purple from his lips and with a shriek he fell in the dust,
biting the ground and drumming with his feet.
The suitor lords flung up their hands and died of laughing . . .

(XVIII, 89–99)

Now the arrogant suitors, in uproarious high spirits, regale the victorious Ulysses like a prince. They pay no attention to the accusations and warnings uttered by the defeated beggarman.

Athene in the meanwhile has advised the sage Penelope to show herself to the suitors in the banqueting hall, where she is to beguile them with deceptive words and inflame them still further. Athene herself helps to deck out the queen and lends her a beauty like that of the Immortals.

55

The fairest of women went down from her shining upper room
(not by herself, for the two maids attended her)
till she reached the suitors. She took her stand by the great column
which upheld the roof; she spread her bright head-veil before her face.
One to either side stood the trusted maids.
The vision of such loveliness enfeebled her courtiers' knees
and filched away their hearts with desire.
Each man prayed that his might be the luck to lie abed with her. (XVIII, 207–212)

Penelope, with prudent intent, tells the suitors of Ulysses' departure twenty years before, and how the departing king had permitted her, if he did not return, to take a new husband as soon as their son Telemachus was grown to manhood. The moment has now come, Penelope says, casting friendly smiles around. And she adds resourcefully that much as it pains her to say so, she must confess that none of the suitors has yet brought her presents, as custom commands. The suitors send their heralds in great haste to fetch regal presents, which they then give to the noble Penelope. She returns to her room, while Ulysses is cheered by the prudence of his loving and faithful wife.

The suitors betake themselves once more to singing and dancing. They make fun of the beggarman, Ulysses, and provoke him continually with arrogant words. And the jeers are taken up by the maidservants who are not loyal to the queen, but dally slyly with the suitors. Telemachus at last brings the banquet to an end, cutting off also the quarrel with the beggarman, by dismissing the suitors to their quarters for the night.

THE PALACE BY NIGHT

Only the godlike Ulysses remains behind with Telemachus in the hall. He bids his son to help him clear the hall of weapons, to leave nothing that the suitors can turn to, when the hour of vengeance strikes. This task accomplished, Ulysses tells Telemachus to sleep. He waits alone in the hall, where Penelope wishes to speak to him. When the queen appears, looking as beautiful as Artemis or Aphrodite, the maidservant Melantho began again to insult him and to order him out of the palace. But Ulysses warns her that the king will soon be back, and Penelope bids the saucy woman leave the hall. Then the queen and beggarman sit down by the fire and Penelope begins to question the traveler. But the wily Ulysses tells her the same story which he had told to the herdsman Eumaeus, a skillful mixture of true adventures and invention. Penelope is moved by the story of the supposed beggarman, who has once, as he says, given shelter to Ulysses.

As he spun them his lies took on the hue of truth;
and as she listened, her tears rained down till her being utterly dissolved,
as the snow laid upon the lofty peaks by the west wind
melts before the breath of the south-easter
and streams down to fill the water-brooks.
So did her fair cheeks stream with grief for the husband
who was sitting beside her in the flesh.

The pictures on the following pages show:

Even Ulysses pitied his unhappy wife, but crafty purpose
kept his eyes hard, with never a tremor to break their steady stare
from eyelids that might have been of horn or iron. (XIX, 203–212)

Questioned by the lovely Penelope, Ulysses also describes exactly how Ulysses was dressed.
Penelope recognizes the description of her own handiwork, and weeps despairingly. Ulysses tries
to console her, predicting that the king will soon return. But Penelope is too disheartened to give
credence to his words. She calls the servant girls and tells them to wash the beggarman's feet. In
the morning, they are to give him a bath and massage him with oil.

Ulysses says, however, that he would prefer to have his feet washed by some old and intelligent
woman. And Penelope tells Eurycleia, an aged nursemaid, to look after the stranger. Eurycleia
had in fact nursed Ulysses as a child, which was why he wished to make trial of her. But fearing
that she would recognize him too soon by an old scar on his leg, he drew back into the shadows
of the fireplace. The old woman had indeed already noticed how like Ulysses the beggarman was.
The old woman saw the scar when she bent near in her washing. . .

Now as the old woman took up his leg and stroked her hands gently
along it she knew the scar by its feel. She let go the foot,
which with his shin splashed down into the tub and upset it
instantly with a noisy clatter. The water poured over the ground.
In Eurycleia's heart such joy and sorrow fought for mastery
that her eyes filled with tears and her voice was stifled in her throat.
So she caught Ulysses by the beard to whisper,
"You are my own child, Ulysses himself, and I never knew —
not till I had fondled the body of my king."
Her eyes travelled across to Penelope,
meaning to signal that her beloved husband was at home:
but Penelope failed to meet this glance or read its meaning,
because Athene momently drew her thought away. Ulysses' right hand
shot out, feeling for Eurycleia's throat, and tightened about it. (XIX, 392, 467–480)

So the noble Ulysses ordered the faithful old woman to keep silence and not betray his return,
promising that he would soon take vengeance on the suitors.

Penelope now approaches the beggarman again, and tells a dream fraught with omens. She
had seen an eagle flying down from the mountain and killing her twenty fat geese. In the dream,
she wept for their loss, and the eagle flew back and told her that the dream was a sign from the
gods. The geese stood for the suitors and the eagle for Ulysses, who was to come back and wreak
fearful vengeance on the suitors. But the prudent Penelope dared not trust her dream and take
new hope. She said to the beggarman:

"Let me tell you something to bear in mind. Presently will dawn
the illfamed day which severs me from the house of Ulysses.
To introduce it I am staging a contest with those axes my lord
(when at home) used to set up, all twelve together,

57

like an alley of oaken bilge-blocks,
before standing well back to send an arrow through the lot.
Now I will put this same feat to my suitors:
and the one who easiest strings the bow with his bare hands
and shoots through the twelve axes, after him will I go,
forsaking this house of my marriage, this very noble, well-appointed house
that surely I shall remember, after, in my dreams."

Ulysses uttered his opinion again:
"August wife of Ulysses, do not hesitate to arrange this trial in the hall;
for Ulysses of the many sleights will be here before those men,
for all their pawing of the shapely bow,
shall have strung it and shot the arrow through the gallery of iron." (XIX, 570–587)

Then Penelope goes to her room, and Athene sends her a refreshing sleep as she weeps. But Ulysses cannot sleep. He is too deeply vexed by the shameful deeds committed in his palace. Then he says to himself, as his anger burns:

"Be patient, heart. You stood a grimmer trial,
that day the bestial Cyclops devoured my splendid fellows.
Steadfastly you bore it, till your cunning had frayed you
a path from that cave you thought your death-trap." (XX, 18–21)

But Athene came and bent over the sleepless hero, consoling him and promising him the aid of the gods. Then she sent Ulysses also a refreshing sleep.

THE RIVAL ARCHERS

With the first light of the following day the servants begin to make ready the hall for the banquet and for the contest among the archers. The swineherd Eumaeus brings down from the hills three pigs which are to be slaughtered for the meal. He gives the beggarman a friendly greeting, while Melanthius, as on the previous day, has only contempt for the stranger and insults him once more with offensive words. The neatherd Philoetius behaves differently. He addresses some friendly words to the beggarman. Ulysses marks well both the insults and the kindly greetings.

During the banquet, the sorely tried Ulysses is seated near the door and receives his due share of all the food. But the suitors take up again their mockery of the beggarman. The goddess Pallas Athene spurs them on, to inflame Ulysses' heart with even fiercer rage. The bold young suitor Ctesippus jeers at the beggarman and ironically promises him a very special gift.

Therewith he snatched a cow's foot from the dish before him
and hurled it with a strong hand: but Ulysses
inclined his head lightly to one side and avoided it, with a wry smile.

58

It crashed harmlessly against the solid wall.

    Telemachus was up to rate Ctesippus soundly.

He cried, "Very profitable for your peace of mind, Ctesippus,

that you missed the stranger! Had he not dodged your shot

I should have thrust you through the midriff with my war-spear

and given your father the pains of your funeral, not your marriage, here.

Let me finally warn you all against displaying violence in my house.

I used to be a child; but have now come

to the knowledge of good and evil."

(XX, 299–310)

The suitors are silenced by Telemachus' courageous words. But then they begin again to make their demands. Telemachus is to order his mother to choose at last one of the suitors. Telemachus wisely answers that while he will not stand in his mother's way if she chooses a new husband, he will never use compulsion on her.

    Their minds clouded by Pallas Athene, the suitors suddenly burst into hoarse laughter, their faces distorted by horrible grimaces. They snatch at the meat and devour it raw, and though they are laughing, they are filled with misery. And now the seer Theoclymenus receives a warning in a waking dream. The coming disaster looms before his eyes, as he sees the walls of the palace covered with blood and all the revelers struck down. This he tells the suitors, but they laugh at him and continue to drink and make merry, while the seer leaves the place in haste and Ulysses sits there silently, waiting for the moment of his dire vengeance.

    Meanwhile Penelope has gone to the treasure house of the great palace, to fetch Ulysses' bow. She now enters the banqueting hall and addresses her arrogant suitors.

"Hear me, my lords and courtiers that have haunted

and beset this house and eaten and drunk here all the long time

the master has been away,

with only excuse and burden of talk your lustful desire

to wed me and possess me for wife.

Now, my suitors, see your test plain.

Here I set the huge bow of godlike Ulysses.

Whoso easiest strings the bow with bare hands

and shoots an arrow through the twelve axes –

after him will I follow, forsaking this house . . ."

(XXI, 68–77)

Telemachus is the first to seize his father's bow. Three times he tries in vain to stretch the bow. He might perhaps have succeeded at the fourth attempt, but his father gives him a secret sign. He replaces the bow and sits down. One by one, the suitors then try to stretch the bow. But none succeeds, though they warm the bow at the fire and rub it with fat to make it more supple. The only ones who have not yet tried to bend the bow are Antinous and Eurymachus, the leaders of the suitors, with their strongest companions.

THE VENGEANCE OF ULYSSES

At this moment, the two herdsmen leave the hall, Philoetius the cattleman and the swineherd Eumaeus. Ulysses follows them quickly, to reassure himself again of their loyalty. He asks them whose side they would take if it came to a fight between their old master, Ulysses, and the interloping suitors. Both have only one wish – that the absent Ulysses should return, so that they can help him to take vengeance on the suitors. When they have thus reaffirmed their loyalty, Ulysses at last reveals the truth, saying:

"But I am back again, my own true self,
here at home after twenty years of hardship . . .
Now I will show you a sure and certain sign,
to make you credit me from the bottom of your hearts.
See my scar, given me by the boar's white tusk so long ago,
as I went upon Parnassus with the sons of Autolycus."
    As he spoke he opened his rags to betray the great scar:
and when the pair of them had studied it and knew it for sure,
they wept and flung their arms about Ulysses,
with most loving kisses for his head and shoulders. (XXI, 207–208, 217–225)

Then the godlike hero discloses his plan for the destruction of the suitors. Eumaeus, the swineherd, is to see that the doors to the inner rooms of the palace are closed. The maidservants are not to be allowed to open them, no matter what noises and shouts they hear. And then the noble swineherd is to hand Ulysses his bow, even against the protests of the arrogant suitors. And the resourceful Ulysses tells the neatherd Philoetius that his task will be to bolt securely the main door of the great hall and keep watch there. Then the herdsmen, with Ulysses in his beggarman's guise, go back once more to the banqueting hall.
    Here the mighty Eurymachus has just tried in vain to bend the bow. He calls out angrily:

"Alas, I sorrow for my own sake and for the general!
It is bitter to forfeit this marriage, yet that is not the worst.
There are plenty more Achaean women here in sea-girt Ithaca,
and others in other cities. What I chiefly regret
is our appearing to fall so short of godlike Ulysses in strength
as not to be able even to bend his bow. The tale will disgrace us generations hence." (XXI, 249–255)

But the crafty Antinous now cries out that today is a feast of the god Apollo, the bender of the bow. It is a day on which no arrows may fly. Tomorrow they will sacrifice to the god and finish the competition. The suitors gladly accept the proposal. But the resourceful Ulysses addresses them with the words:

"Hear me, suitors of the famous queen,
while I retail the promptings of my heart, making my main appeal to Eurymachus,
and to godlike Antinous for his fitting counsel

60

just now to leave the bow to the gods' reference.
In the morning the god will give mastery to whom he wills.
Yet for the moment pass me this polished bow that I may test
my hands and strength while you watch, to see whether there yet
lies in me the virtue that once inhabited my supple limbs,
or if the privations of a wandering life have wasted it right away."
   His words enraged them all and instantly . . .

(XXI, 275–285)

   But the sage Penelope responds with mockery to the raging words of Antinous. Is the noble suitor perhaps afraid that the miserable beggarman will succeed in bending the bow and in winning her as his bride? Penelope gives orders that the stranger be also allowed to try his strength on the bow. But the noble Telemachus tells his mother that he alone can dispose of his father's heritage, the bow. And then, in his concern for his mother, he bids her leave the hall.

   Then the swineherd Eumaeus takes the bow and brings it to the beggarman, with the suitors all protesting loudly, but encouraged by the noble Telemachus. Ulysses had already told the faithful Eurycleia to close the inner doors, and the neatherd Philoetius had bolted the main door of the hall, as he had been ordered. Ulysses first tests the bow carefully, to see that it has not suffered damage during his long absence. Then, with an easy movement, almost negligently, he bends the bow.

   Changing the bow to his right hand he proved the string,
which sang to his pluck, sharp like a swallow's cry.
Distress overwhelmed the suitors and they changed colour.
Zeus declared himself in a loud thunder-peal;
and long-suffering royal Ulysses rejoiced
that the son of devious-counselled Cronos should make him a sign.
He snatched up the keen arrow which lay naked there upon his table –
all the others which the Achaeans were so soon to feel
being yet stored in their quiver –
and set it firmly upon the grip of the bow.
He notched it to the string and drew;
and from his place upon his settle, just as he sat,
sent the arrow with so straight an aim that he did not foul one single axe.
The bronze-headed shaft threaded through clean,
from the leading helve onward
till it issued through the portal of the last ones.

(XXI, 410–423)

   Then the sorely tried Ulysses cries out proudly to his son: "You see that my strength is not impaired and that I am not as feeble as these suitors said when they derided me." Telemachus then quickly seizes his sword and his lance and takes his place at his father's side. Ulysses casts away his beggarman's cloak, leaps up on the high threshold of the hall, shakes the winged arrows from his quiver onto the ground at his feet and cries out to the suitors, who are frozen with terror:

"At last, at last the ending of this fearful strain!
Before me, by favour of Apollo if my luck holds,
stands a virgin target never yet hit."
He levelled the bitter arrow at Antinous
whose two hands were raising the splendid golden wine-cup
to his lips, without suspicion of death in his heart –
for who, at a thronged banquet, could conceive of any single man
being bold enough to dare compass his violent death
and bloody destruction? However Ulysses shot,
and took him with the shaft full in the throat.
Right through his graceful neck and out again went the point.
He rolled over sideways, letting the cup fall
from his stricken grasp and thrusting back the table
with a jerk of his foot that threw his food,
the bread and the cooked meats, to pollution on the floor.
The life-blood spurted thickly from his nostrils.
    One outcry broke through the house from the suitors
when they saw the man fall. They sprang in terror
from their thrones, and gaped all about.
                            (XXII, 5–23)

The terrified suitors search in vain for weapons. Ulysses and Telemachus had long ago emptied
the hall of its armory. And the suitors hurl insults and threats at the marksman, still thinking
that it was only by accident that he had hit Antinous.

    But Ulysses glaring at them cried, "Dogs that you are, you kept
harping on your conviction that I would never return
from the Troad, and in that strong belief let yourselves ravage my house . . .
Now you are all trapped in death's toils."
                            (XXII, 33–35, 40)

Eurymachus, the suitors' other leader, now tries to placate Ulysses' anger, craftily trying to
put all the blame for the suitors' misdeeds on the dead Antinous. It was all in vain.
There was no softening of that glare as Ulysses rejoined:

"Eurymachus, not if you gave away to me your whole inheritance,
all that you now own and yet may earn, would I relax my hands
from slaughtering until the suitors have paid the last jot
for their presumptions. Only flight or fight confront you now
as escapes from ultimate death: and some of you, I think,
will find no way of avoiding doom's abyss."
                            (XXII, 60–68)

And now Eurymachus, seeing no other escape, spurs on his companions to attack Ulysses.   62

He himself draws his two-edged sword and rushes at Ulysses with a fierce cry. But Ulysses looses another arrow and Eurymachus falls. Telemachus' lance pierces another suitor who tries to avenge the death of his leader. He then hastens to the armory and fetches helmets and shields and eight sharp spears for himself and his father and the two loyal herdsmen. But Ulysses, as long as he has arrows for his bow, lays low a suitor with every shot.

But when the royal archer had no arrows left he put
the bow aside against a polished return of the massive hall-entrance,
while he passed a four-ply shield over his shoulders
and dressed his great head in a close-fitting helmet,
grim under the towering menace of its nodding horse-hair crest.
He took up two brave bronze-pointed spears.
(XXII, 119–125)

Suddenly the hero sees that the suitors are also arming themselves. The goatherd, the crafty treacherous Melanthius, had stolen into the armory through a small door which Eumaeus should have guarded, and had fetched weapons and armor for the suitors. Ulysses at once bids the two loyal herdsmen to follow the traitor, who has slipped back into the armory, and tie him securely.

Pallas Athene now joins the fighters in the hall, encouraging Ulysses and diverting the spears thrown by the suitors. Only Telemachus and the swineherd Eumaeus receive light flesh wounds in the murderous struggle. And Athene, encouraging once more Ulysses and his faithful allies, shakes her thundering shield. The suitors are panic-stricken, and scatter throughout the hall.

Like that were the suitors buffeted every way up and down the hall,
while the dismal crunch of cracking skulls increased
and the whole floor seeped with blood.
(XXII, 307–309)

Ulysses keeps up his merciless onslaught, till all the suitors lie dead on the ground. Only the singer Phemius and the herald Medon are spared by his anger, at the plea of Telemachus. Ulysses then sends Telemachus to fetch his old nurse, the faithful Eurycleia. He has an errand for her. The old lady follows the king's son into the hall, as fast as she can.

She opened the doors of the stately hall and paced in
(Telemachus ushering her) to where Ulysses stood in a slaver of blood
and muck amidst the corpses of his victims,
like some lion that has devoured an ox at grass and prowls forth,
terrible to the eye, with gory breast and chaps.
So was Ulysses bedabbled from his hands right down to his feet.
She, when she saw the corpses and the pools of blood,
knew how great was the achievement and opened her mouth to raise
the woman's battle-wail: but Ulysses checked her excitement . . .
(XXII, 401–408)

Ulysses forbids Eurycleia to give vent to her joy. It is a sin to gloat over slaughtered men. He asks his loyal nurse which of the maidservants have been unfaithful. Eurycleia names twelve, out of the fifty maids-in-waiting in the great palace. These twelve are then forced by Ulysses to clean the hall, to carry out the dead, and to wash away the blood from the tables and benches. And when they have finished this gruesome task, Telemachus takes them out into the courtyard, and hangs them on a hawser which he loops round each of their necks.

Sometimes in a shrubbery men so stretch out nets, upon which
long-winged thrushes or doves alight on their way to roost:
and fatal the perch proves. Exactly thus were the women's
heads all held a-row with a bight of cord drawn round each throat,
to suffer their caitiff's death. A little while they twittered
with their feet – only a little. It was not long.
(XXII, 468–473)

Then the treacherous goatherd Melanthius meets his due punishment at the hands of Telemachus and the angry herdsmen. He is savagely mutilated and then thrown to the dogs to be devoured. Meanwhile Ulysses takes precautions against malediction by fumigating the hall with sulfur. Then he tells the faithful Eurycleia that the time has come for her to call Penelope and her maids.

ULYSSES AND PENELOPE

The fearsome work of vengeance is thus successfully finished. And the old lady hurries away to Penelope's room, where she is deep in a sleep sent by Athene. Eurycleia, beaming with joy, wakes the sleeping queen with her cry:

"Awake dear child, Penelope:
open your eyes upon the sight you have yearned for all these days.
Ulysses has appeared, at this end of time.
He has reached his home and in it slaughtered
the recalcitrant suitors who for so long vexed the house,
ate his stored wealth and outfaced his son."
(XXIII, 5–9)

But Penelope cannot credit the old lady's message. Even when Eurycleia tells her of the unmistakable sign, Ulysses' scar, Penelope remains in the grip of doubt. But she follows the old nurse down to the hall, and sits down in her chair by the fire, facing Ulysses, who is resting by one of the pillars. And still she says nothing, gazing at the hero, thinking for a moment that she recognizes him, and then again hesitating, as she sees the beggarly rags in which he is clad.

And now Telemachus tells his mother to go and sit by the stranger, to put him questions and satisfy herself at last that the wanderer has come home. Indignant, he cries out to Penelope:

The pictures on the following pages show:

"No other woman could in cold blood keep herself apart,
when her man got home after twenty years of toil and sorrow.
Your heart remains harder than a stone."
But Penelope explained: "Child, my heart is dazed.
I have no force to speak, or ask, or even stare upon his face.
If this is Ulysses in truth and at last, then shall we soon know
each other better than well by certain private signs between us two,
hidden from the rest of the world."
(XXIII, 100–110)

But Ulysses only smiles, and lets Penelope have her way. First he tells his son to take his bath and dress himself as for a feast. Then the minstrel is to strike up a gay tune, so that the sounds from the hall will convince the townsfolk that the suitor's feasting is still going on. The possible supporters of the suitors are to learn nothing as yet of the vengeance that has overtaken the princes of Ithaca. So the servants join in the song and the dance, while Ulysses has himself bathed and rubbed with fragrant oils. Then, with a new strength lent him by the goddess Athene, and radiant with a divine charm, he makes his way back to Penelope, looking like one of the immortal gods. But the sage lady puts him to the severest test. She tells the old nurse to make up the king's bed so that he can rest, but outside the bedroom which Ulysses himself had built long ago. But when Ulysses had been at work, he had built the bed into the trunk of a mighty olive-tree, a bed post well rooted in the earth. So the bed cannot possibly be moved. When Penelope gives the wily command, Ulysses flames up in anger and turns on his noble wife:

"Woman, this order pains my heart. Who has changed my bed?
It would task the cunningest man – forbye no god happened
to shift it in whim – for not the stoutest wight alive
could heave it up directly. That bed's design
held a marvellous feature of my own contriving . . ."
As Ulysses had run on, furnishing her with proof too solid
for rejection, her knees trembled, and her heart.
She burst into tears, she ran to him, she flung her arms
about his neck and kissed his head and cried,
"My Ulysses, forgive me this time too,
you who were of old more comprehending than any man of men.
The gods gave us sorrow for our portion,
and in envy denied us the happiness of being together
throughout our days, from the heat of youth to the shadow of old age.
Be not angry with me, therefore, nor resentful,
because at first sight I failed to fondle you thus."
(XXIII, 183–189, 205–214)

Thus finally united in love, Ulysses and Penelope pass the night together, and the much-tried wanderer tells her of all his adventures and sufferings on his long way home.
The next morning, Ulysses sets out for the country estate, where his father the old king Laertes

is living, to see him once more and bring him the good news of his happy return and the terrible punishment of the suitors. He finds the old man, dressed in the simple clothes of a gardener, busy in his orchard. But first the wily Ulysses seeks to sound out his father's mind, by spinning him tales which are only half-true. But as he sees how deeply his father is mourning for his lost son, he finally tells the grief-stricken ancient the whole truth.

He leaped forward and caught him in his arms and kissed him, crying,
"I, my father, I myself am the one you ask after,
arrived in this twentieth year at home. Cease your sighs and sobs . . ."

(XXIV, 319–322)

Having convinced his father by unimpeachable proofs, Ulysses leads him to the house, where Telemachus and the herdsmen have prepared a splendid banquet. They sit down, talking gaily to celebrate the happy reunion.

THE LAST FIGHT

The news of the extreme punishment which Ulysses, with the help of only a few loyal companions, had meted out to the suitors, has in the meantime spread rapidly in the town, and the citizens, headed by the fathers of the slain, hurry to the market place, to hold an official assembly. The first to speak was Eupeithes, the father of the luckless Antinous, the first to fall under Ulysses' arrows.

Tears rained from his eyes as he harangued them, saying, "O my friends,
the vast mischief this man has worked against the Achaeans!
Think of the many stout warriors he took aboard with him,
only to cast away his ships and all their crews; while he returns only
to butcher the very best leaders of the Cephallenians that remained.
You must act before he takes swift flight to Pylos or to sacred Elis,
the Epeian sanctuary. Let us forward, or our faces will be for ever bowed with shame.
The disgrace of it will echo down the generations,
should we fail to punish the murderers of your sons and kinsmen.
For me, there would remain no sweetness in life.
Rather would I choose death and the company of these dead.
Up and strike, before they steal from us oversea."

(XXIV, 424–436)

But only half of the assembly responds to this call for vengeance on Ulysses. The minstrel and the herald, who owe their lives to Ulysses' mercy, intervene to tell the astonished crowd how a god had stood by Ulysses to help him inflict the just punishment. Not to anger the god, half **66** of the assembly hurries home in terror. The others arm themselves and march out, with Eupeithes at their head, to do battle with Ulysses.

On Mount Olympus, however, Zeus and his grey-eyed daughter Athene are discussing the threat of fratricidal wars in Ithaca. And Zeus tells his daughter to see to it that all ends happily, with Ulysses secure on his royal throne. Athene speeds to earth in a mighty swoop from high Olympus, and goes to the farm of the old king, Laertes, where the meal is just ending.

But the watchful Ulysses already senses the coming of the enemy. In haste, he arms his son and his old father, and also the loyal herdsmen and the six sons of the faithful Dolius, the steward who farms Laertes' land. And Athene fills the handful of warriors with courage for the fray.

With the first cast of his lance, the grey-haired Laertes kills the leader of the hostile band, Eupeithes, as he rushes on breathing vengeance. It is enough to throw the attackers into confusion and to encourage Laertes' companions.

Ulysses and his brave son fell upon the leading rank,
hacking with their swords and thrusting with their spears.
They would have cut them off and destroyed every one had not Athene,
the daughter of aegis-bearing Zeus,
shouted with such force as to halt the array.
"Let be your deadly battle, men of Ithaca," she cried.
"Without bloodshed is the affair best arranged."
The voice of the goddess blenched them with fear.
In their panic the weapons slipped from their grasp
and fell together to the ground, as the goddess called.
They turned their faces toward the town for dear life,
while with a roar the great long-suffering Ulysses
gathered himself for the spring
and launched after them, like an eagle in free air.
But instantly the son of Cronos flung his lurid levin
which fell before the grey-eyed goddess,
the dread Father's own child; then did Athene cry to Ulysses,
"Back with you, heaven-nourished son of Laertes,
Ulysses of the many wiles. Hold back.
Cease this arbitrament of civil war.
Move not far-sighted Zeus to wrath."
So Athene said, she the daughter of aegis-bearing Zeus.
Ulysses obeyed, inwardly glad: and Pallas,
still with Mentor's form and voice, set a pact between them
for ever and ever.
(XXIV, 525–547)

These are the lines with which the poet Homer ends his story of the adventures and the happy return of the godlike Ulysses, who was to live long as king over Ithaca when the strife was ended, united in love with the faithful Penelope.

67

INDEX OF PLATES AND
BIBLIOGRAPHY

1 GREEK SINGERS. Bronze statuette from the geometric period. Height: 2.15 in. — Iraklion, Archaeological Museum, Inv. 2064.

2 HEAD OF ATHENE. Statue of Parian marble. From the Palazzo Mattei, Rome, later in the Fesch collection. Acquired by Louis XVIII. Roman copy of a Greek original (Athena Agoraia?) from the second half of the 4th cent. B.C. Height: 7 ft. 6 in. — Paris, Louvre, Inv. 530.

Lit.: W. Fröhner, *Notice de la Sculpture Antique du Musée Impérial du Louvre* I (Paris 1869), No. 121. — Charles Picard, *Manuel de la Sculpture* IV, 2, 1 (Paris 1963), p. 368. — Giulio Emanuele Rizzo, *Prassitele* (Milano 1932), p. 118, pl. 143.

3 ULYSSES. Bronze statuette. Roman period. Height: 4 ft. 7 in. — Paris, Bibliothèque Nationale, Inv. 809.

Lit.: Ernest Babelon – J.-Adrien Blanchet, *Cat. des bronzes antiques de la Bibliothèque Nationale* (Paris 1895), p. 349, 809. — Heinrich Heydemann, *Pariser Antiken* (1887), p. 69, 11.

4 OLYMPUS. A mountainous mass of many peaks, seen from the sea. The highest elevation in Greece, Mt Olympus (9568 feet) forms the border between Thessaly and Macedonia. It was regarded in antiquity as the dwelling-place of the gods.

5 ZEUS ENTHRONED. Bronze statuette from Mt Lycaeum in Arcadia, probably Zeus Lycaeus. Corinthian, second half of the 6th cent. B.C. Height: 4 in. — Athens, National Museum, Inv. 13209.

Lit.: K. Kourouniotis, *Archaiologiké Ephemerís* 24 (1904), pp. 185ff. Fig. 12–14. — V. Stais, *Marbres et Bronzes du Musée National* (Athens, 1909–10), p. 314. — Ernst Langlotz, *Frühgriechische Bildhauerschulen* (Nuremberg 1927), p. 80, pl. 41b.

6 POSEIDON. Bronze statue, from the sea at Cape Artemisium, found without the arms, 1926; the arms found 1928. Second quarter of the 5th cent. B.C. Height: 6 ft. 10 in. — Athens, National Museum, Inv. 15161.

Lit.: Charles Picard, *Manuel de la Sculpture* II, 1 (Paris 1939), pp. 63ff., p. 14 and 14 *bis*. — Reinhard Lullies – Max Hirmer, *Griechische Plastik* (Munich 1960), pp. 58ff., pl. 130–2.

7 MISSION OF ATHENE. Cameo from the Becken collection, presented to the Bibliothèque Nationale in 1846. Roman period. Size: 1.3 × 1.2 in. — Paris, Bibliothèque Nationale, Inv. 3.

Lit.: Ernest Babelon, *Le Cabinet des Médailles et Antiques* (Paris 1924), p. 167, 3.

8 ATHENE. Marble statue from Crete. End of the 5th cent. B.C. Height: 4 ft. 6 in. — Paris, Louvre, Inv. 847.

Lit.: *Encyclopédie Photographique* III (Paris), p. 181. — Charles Picard, *Manuel de la Sculpture* II, 2, p. 550, fig. 225. — E. Reisch, *Jahreshefte des österreichischen archäologischen Instituts* 1 (1898), pp. 72ff., fig. 35.

9 ITHACA. View from the coast road near Stavros. The harbour in the Odyssey was in the bay, and the market-place was on the mountain-ridge. As late as the first cent. B.C., Ulysses was worshipped as a hero in a small cave on the shore of the headland.

10 PENELOPE MOURNING. Terracotta relief. Roman period. Height: 10 in.; length: 10.5 in. — London, British Museum, Cat. D 609 (Towneley Collection).

Lit.: H. B. Walters, *Cat. of the Terracottas in the British Museum* (London 1903), p. 403, 609.

11 PYLOS. Entrance to the bay of Navarino on the west coast of the Peloponnese. About a mile from the coast are the ruins of the palace of King Nestor, from Mycenaean times.

12 TELEMACHUS AND NESTOR. Red-figured bowl from Lower Italy, 4th cent. B.C. Acquired in Naples in 1849. Height: 20 in. — Berlin, Staatliche Museen (Charlottenburg), Inv. (of the Antiquarium) 3289.

Lit.: Adolf Furtwängler, *Beschreibung der Vasensammlung im Antiquarium* (Berlin 1885), p. 922, 3289.

13 AGAMEMNON. Gold mask from Tomb V, Mycenae. 16th cent. B.C. Excavated by Heinrich Schliemann. Height: 10 in. — Athens, National Museum, Inv. 624.

Lit.: Georg Karo, *Die Schachtgräber von Mykenai,* 2 vols (Munich 1930–3), fig. in text p. 18. — Spyridon Marinatos – Max Hirmer, *Kreta und das mykenische Hellas* (Munich 1959), p. 115, pl. 162. — Friedrich Matz, *Kreta, Mykene, Troja* (Stuttgart 1956), p. 272, pl. 87.

14 KING NESTOR'S BATH. Clay, about 1200 B.C. Excavated in the palace of Pylos in 1955 by the American archaeologist Carl W. Blegen. Length: *c.* 5 ft. 10 in.; width: *c.* 2 ft. 4 in.

Lit.: Carl W. Blegen, *American Journal of Archaeology* 60 (1956), p. 100, pl. 47, fig. 20–21.

15 BULL WITH GOLDEN HORNS. A rhyton of silver and gold from Tomb IV in Mycenae. 16th cent. B.C. Height: 12 in. — Athens, National Museum, Inv. 384.

Lit.: Helmuth T. Bossert, *Altkreta* (Berlin 1937), p. 22, pl. 96. — Spyridon Marinatos – Max Hirmer, *Kreta und das mykenische Hellas* (Munich 1959), p. 117, pl. 175. — Friedrich Matz, *Kreta und frühes Griechenland* (Baden-Baden 1962), p. 172.

16 VIEW TOWARDS SPARTA. Telemachus must have looked from the top of this pass onto the plain of Lacedaemonia. The pass forms the boundary between Messenia and Lacedaemonia, as is proved by an ancient boundary stone found on the site.

17 MENELAUS AND HELEN. Etruscan bronze mirror, 4th cent. B.C. Height: 10.5 in.; diameter: 6.7 in. — London, British Museum, Cat. 712 (Towneley Collection).

Lit.: H. B. Walters, *Cat. of the Bronzes in the British Museum* (London 1899), p. 120, 712. — Eduard Gerhard, *Etruskische Spiegel* II (Berlin 1843–97), pl. 201, III, p. 194.

18 ULYSSES CREEPING. Marble statue from Rome, found in 1885. An archaizing Roman work of about A.D. 50. Height: 2 ft. 1 in.; length: 3 ft. 8 in. — Boston, Mrs Stewart Gardner Museum.

Lit.: R. Lanciani, *Notizie degli Scavi* (1885), p. 341. — V. Poulsen, *Acta Archaeologica* 25 (1954), pp. 301 ff.

19 THE ISLAND OF ASTERIS, where the suitors lay in wait for Telemachus in the strait between Ithaca and Cephalonia, seen from Ithaca. The island is now called Dascalion.

23 PHAEACIAN COAST. The island of Corfu, the ancient Scheria, was already regarded in antiquity as the country of the Phaeacians. The bay of Ermonais in the foreground, which is the only sandy beach on the whole west coast of Corfu where a river flows into the sea, corresponds exactly to Homer's description of Ulysses' landing-place.

20 HERMES. Bronze statuette from Mt Lycaeum (Arcadia). Beginning of the 5th cent. B.C. Height (without base): 5 in. — Athens, National Museum, Inv. 13219.

Lit.: K. Kourouniotis, *Archaiologiké Ephemerís* 24 (1904), pp. 196 ff., pl. 9. — V. Stais, *Marbres et Bronzes du Musée National* (Athens 1909–10), p. 317, 13219.

24 ULYSSES AND ATHENE at the meeting with Nausicaa. Attic red-figured amphora by the Nausicaa-painter, from Vulci. About 450–440 B.C. Height: 20 in. — Munich, Museum antiker Kleinkunst, Inv. 2322.

Lit.: Friedrich Hauser, *Jahreshefte des österreichischen archäologischen Institutes* 8 (1905), p. 27. — J. D. Beazley, *Attic Red-figured Vase-Painters* II (Oxford 1963), p. 1107, 2. — Reinhard Lullies, *Corpus Vasorum Antiquorum Munich* 5, pp. 9–11, pl. 213.

25 THE GROVE OF ATHENE, a little before the double inlet of Paleocastrizza, on the road from Ermonais through the plain of Ropas.

21 ULYSSES AND CALYPSO. Red-figured Ralpis (type of hydria) from Paestum, S. Italy. Last quarter of the 5th cent. B.C. Height: *c.* 20 in. — Naples, Museo Nazionale, Cat. 2899.

Lit.: Heinrich Heydemann, *Die Vasensammlungen des Museo Nazionale* (Berlin 1872), No. 2899. — Festa, *Rendiconti dell'Acc. dei Lincei* 21 (1912), pp. 383 ff.

26 PROVISION JAR in the cellar of the royal palace of Cnossos. 15th century B.C. Height: *c.* 5 ft. 4 in.

Lit.: Arthur Evans, *The Palace of Minos* IV (London 1921–36), pp. 630 ff. — Spyridon Marinatos – Max Hirmer, *Kreta und das mykenische Hellas* (Munich 1959), p. 78, pl. 41.

22 STORM AT SEA. Poseidon, the sea-god, shows his anger towards Ulysses by bringing a furious gale that buffets him for two days and two nights off the Phaeacian coast.

27 THE PHAEACIANS' BANQUET in honour of Ulysses. Attic red-figured bowl. Second quarter of the 5th. cent. B.C. Since 1814 in the Kunsthistorisches Museum, Vienna. Height: 18 in.; width: 17 in. — Vienna, Kunsthistorisches Museum, Inv. 824.

Lit.: Fritz Eichler, *Corpus Vasorum Antiquorum Vienna, Kunsthistorisches Museum* 2, p. 27, pl. 89.

28 YOUNG ACHAEANS AT THE ATHLETIC CONTESTS. Relief in Pentelic marble from a square pedestal. Found 1922 in a wall at the Dipylon, Athens. Probably part of the base of a statue. 510–500 B.C. Height: 12.8 in.; length: 32 in. — Athens, National Museum, Inv. 3476.

Lit.: Charles Picard, *Manuel de la Sculpture* I (Paris 1935), pp. 628 ff. — Reinhard Lullies – Max Hirmer, *Griechische Plastik* (Munich 1960), p. 48, pl. 62–65.

29 GREEK SINGERS. Clay statuette from the geometric period. Found in 1924 in the Arcades/Crete. Height: 3 in. — Iraklion, Archaeological Museum, Inv. 8104.

30 TROJAN HORSE. Depicted on the neck of an earthenware amphora with reliefs, from Mykonos, found in 1961. First half of the 7th cent. B.C. Height: 4 ft. — Mykonos, Museum.

Lit.: Georges Daux, *Bulletin de Correspondence Hellénique* 86 (1962), p. 854, fig. 16, pl. 29. — Hans Walter, *Athen. Mitt.* 77 (1962), p. 196. — Karl Schefold, *Frühgriechische Sagenbilder* (Munich 1964), pl. 34.

31 HEAD OF ULYSSES. Fragment of a marble statue from the cave of Tiberius in Sperlonga, middle of the first cent. B.C. (?) Height: 26 in. — Sperlonga, Museum.

Lit.: Giulio Jacopi, *I ritrovamenti dell'antro cosiddetto "di Tiberio" a Sperlonga* (Rome 1958), fig. 10. — Giulio Jacopi, *L'antro di Tiberio a Sperlonga* (Rome 1963), fig. 23, 24, 55–57.

32 THE SEA COAST. Day after day Ulysses sat eyeing the fruitless sea.

33 THE PALM TREES OF THE LOTOS-EATERS. The island of Djerba off the coast of Tunis was already regarded in ancient times as the dwelling-place of the Lotos-eaters of the legend.

34 THE HARBOUR OF THE CYCLOPES. A small bay at the foot of Mt Posillipo, invisible from the landward side.

35 HEAD OF POLYPHEMUS. Terracotta fragment from Smyrna. Hellenistic period. Height: 2 in. — Paris, Louvre, Inv. CA 1003.

36 THE BLINDING OF POLYPHEMUS. Early Attic amphora from Eleusis, found in 1954. Second quarter of the 7th cent. B.C. Height: 4 ft. 4 in. — Eleusis, Museum.

Lit.: G. E. Mylonas, Ὁ πρωτοαττικὸς ἀμφορεὺς τῆς Ἐλευσῖνος (Athens 1957). — Karl Schefold, *Frühgriechische Sagenbilder* (Munich 1964), p. 32, pl. 16, pl. 1.

37 ULYSSES' ESCAPE UNDER THE RAM. Black-figured convex lekythos by the "Ambush-painter", from Girgenti. Last decade of the 6th cent. B.C. Height: c. 10.5 in. — Munich, Antikensammlung, Inv. 1885 (J. 755).

Lit.: Jane E. Harrison, *Journal of Hellenic Studies* 4 (1883), table, p. 259, No. 4. — Emilie Haspels, *Attic Black-figured Lekythoi* (Paris 1936), p. 61.

38 THE ROUTE FROM THE ISLAND OF THE CYCLOPES. The little island of Nisida can be seen from the many caves of Mt Posillipo, most of which were made or enlarged in the time of Augustus. The rocks which Polyphemus threw after Ulysses' ship are in the water in the foreground.

39 POSEIDON. Bronze statuette, second half of the 2nd cent. B.C. Height (to the fingers of the left hand): 12.2 in. — Munich, Antikensammlung, Loeb Collection No. 15.

Lit.: Johannes Sieveking, *Die Bronzen der Sammlung Loeb* (Munich 1913), pp. 41 ff., pl. 17–18. — Charles Picard, *Manuel de la Sculpture* IV, 2 (Paris 1963), pp. 509 f., fig. 208.

40 AEOLUS' WALL OF FIRE. On the northwestern slope of the vulcano on Stromboli, the petrified lava-flow falls very steeply into the sea. It was the gold-bronze coloration of the wall which the ancients recognized as Aeolus' famed wall of fire.

41 THE ISLAND OF AEOLUS. The island of Stromboli, one of the Lipari group, was regarded in antiquity as the seat of Aeolus, the lord of the winds. The volcano on the island, 3038 feet high, is still active.

42 CIRCE'S ISLAND. Monte Circeo on the Gulf of Gaeta, now joined to the mainland by a change in the ocean bed, was already regarded in antiquity as the home of the goddess Circe.

43 CIRCE OFFERS ULYSSES THE MAGIC POTION. Attic black-figured lekythos by the Athene-painter, from Eretria on the island of Euboea. First quarter of the 5th cent. B.C. Height: 11.4 in. — Athens, National Museum, Inv. 1133.

Lit.: Eugénie Sellers, *Journal of Hellenic Studies* 13 (1892), pp. 7 ff. — Emilie Haspels, *Attic Black-figured Lekythoi* (Paris 1936), p. 256,49, pl. 45,6.

44 ULYSSES THREATENING CIRCE. Etruscan sarcophagus relief from Torre S. Severo, found in 1912. Of pepper-tree wood. From the end of the 4th cent. B.C., probably an imitation of a Greek painting of the 5th cent. B.C. Height (with lid): 37 in.; length: 31.5 in. — Orvieto, Museo dell'Opera del Duomo.

Lit.: Edoardo Galli, *Monumenti antichi pubblicati dall'Accademia dei Lincei* 24,1 (1916), pp. 19 ff. — Pericle Ducati – G. Q. Giglioli, *Arte etrusca Scultura* (Rome–Milan 1927), p. 45, fig. 51. — Reinhard Herbig, *Die jüngeretruskischen Steinsarkophage* (Berlin 1952), p. 40, No. 73.

45 LAKE AVERNUS. A water-filled crater north of Pozzuoli, was regarded in antiquity as the dwelling-place of the Cimmerians (Odyssey, Book XI), and as an entrance to the underworld. There are several caves and grottoes on the southern shore, one of which is called the "Cave of the Sibyl". Under Augustus, a canal was cut to join the lake to the Gulf of Pozzuoli.

46 ULYSSES SACRIFICING. Etruscan sarcophagus relief from Torre S. Severo, found in 1912. Of pepper-tree wood. From the end of the 4th cent. B.C., probably an imitation of a Greek painting of the 5th cent. B.C. Height (with lid): 37 in.; length: 31.5 in. — Orvieto, Museo dell'Opera del Duomo.

Lit.: Edoardo Galli, *Monumenti antichi pubblicati dall'Accademia dei Lincei* 24,1 (1916), pp. 19 ff. — Pericle Ducati – C. Q. Gigioli, *Arte etrusca Scultura* (Rome–Milan 1927), p. 45, fig. 51. — Reinhard Herbig, *Die jüngeretruskischen Steinsarkophage* (Berlin 1952), p. 40, No. 73.

47 ULYSSES AND TEIRESIAS. South Italian red-figured bowl, from the Barone collection. End of the 5th cent. B.C. Height (without base): 18.8 in., diameter (at top): 18.8 in. — Paris, Bibliothèque Nationale, Inv. 422 (Luynes 731).

Lit.: A. De Ridder, *Cat. des Vases peints*, p. 312, 422.

48 ULYSSES' SHIP. Campana terracotta relief (much restored and painted over). 2nd cent. A.D., probably from the time of Hadrian. Height: 13 in.; length: 16.1 in. — Paris, Louvre, Inv. 747.

Lit.: H. von Rohden – H. Winnefeld, *Architektonische römische Tonreliefs der Kaiserzeit* (Stuttgart 1911), p. 111, pl. 132. — Franz Müller, *Die antiken Odysseeillustrationen* (Berlin 1913), p. 44.

49 SIREN. Attic red-figured stamnos by the Siren-painter, from Vulci. First quarter of the 5th cent. B.C. Height: 14.1 in. — London, British Museum, Cat. E 440 (Canino Collection 829).

Lit.: C. H. Smith, *Cat. of the Greek and Etruscan Vases in the British Museum* III (London 1896), p. 268, E 440. — *Corpus Vasorum Antiquorum, British Museum* III, Ic, pl. 20, Ic, p. 8. — J. D. Beazley, *Attic Red-figured Vase-Painters* I (Oxford 1963), p. 289,1.

50 SCYLLA'S ROCK guards the Straits of Messina, the narrow channel dividing Italy from Sicily. It is opposite Punta del Faro, the eastern tip of Sicily.

51 SCYLLA'S TAIL. Fragment of a group in marble from the Cave of Tiberius in Sperlonga, found in 1957. Middle of the first cent. B.C. (?) — Sperlonga, Museum.

Lit.: Giulio Jacopi, *L'antro di Tiberio a Sperlonga* (Rome 1963), fig. 38.

52 HAND OF SCYLLA. Fragment of a group in marble from the Cave of Tiberius in Sperlonga, found in 1957. Middle of the first cent. B.C. (?) Height: 8 in.; length: 13.7 in. — Sperlonga, Museum.

Lit.: Giulio Jacopi, *I ritrovamenti dell' antro cosiddetto "di Tiberio" a Sperlonga* (Rome 1958), fig. 6, 16. — Giulio Jacopi, *L'antro di Tiberio a Sperlonga* (Rome 1963), fig. 38.

53 THE OXEN OF THE SUN. Caeretan Hydria from Italy, about 550 B.C. Height: 16.8 in. — Paris, Louvre, Inv. E 702.

Lit.: N. Plaoutine, *Corpus Vasorum Antiquorum, Louvre* III F., p. 9, pl. 8,3.

54 ONE OF ULYSSES' COMPANIONS in despair over the slaughter of the sacred cattle. Bronze statuette from the Acropolis in Athens, found in 1836. 6th cent. B.C. Height: 3.7 in. — Paris, Bibliothèque Nationale, Inv. 811 (Oppermann Collection).

Lit.: Ernest Babelon – J.-Adrien Blanchet, *Cat. des Bronzes antiques de la Bibliothèque Nationale* (Paris 1895), p. 350,811. — H. G. Niemeyer in *Antike Plastik*, Fasc. III, 1, pl. 31 a.

55 CHARYBDIS. There are several whirlpools in the Straits of Messina, which can produce dangerous cross-currents, especially when the wind sets up a strong flow through the straits. The legend of Scylla and Charybdis grew up about these whirlpools. The picture shows the view towards Sicily, with the rock of Scylla.

56 OARSMEN. Attic red-figured stamnos by the Siren-painter, from Vulci. First quarter of the 5th cent. B.C. Height: 14 in. — London, British Museum, Cat. E 440 (Canino Collection 829).

Lit.: C. H. Smith, *Cat. of the Greek and Etruscan Vases in the British Museum* III (London 1896), p. 268, E 440. — *Corpus Vasorum Antiquorum British Museum* III, Ic, pl. 20, Ic, p. 8. — J. D. Beazley, *Attic Red-figured Vase-Painters* I (Oxford 1963), p. 289,1.

57 HEAD OF ULYSSES. Bronze statuette, Roman period (detail of No. 2). Height: 4.7 in. — Paris, Bibliothèque Nationale, Inv. 809.

Lit.: Ernest Babelon – J.-Adrien Blanchet, *Cat. des Bronzes antiques de la Bibliothèque Nationale* (Paris 1895), p. 349,809. — Heinrich Heydemann, *Pariser Antiken* (1887), p. 69,11.

58 ATHENE. Bronze statuette from Aetolia, of provincial workmanship, from the 5th cent. B.C. Height: 8 in. — Paris, Louvre, Cat. 173.

Lit.: A. De Ridder, *Les Bronzes antiques du Louvre* I (Paris 1913), p. 33,173, pl. 18.

59 CAVE OF THE NYMPHS. On Ithaca, about a mile and a half from Ulysses' landing-place on the Bay of Phorkys there is a cave with stalactites, the Cave of the Nymphs, where Ulysses hid the presents given him by the Phaeacians. The entry is narrow, but there is an opening in the roof, "the entrance of the gods".

60 THE PLATEAU OF MARATHIA, in the south of Ithaca, supposed to be the place where Eumaeus, Ulysses' faithful swineherd, kept his herds.

61 EUMAEUS. Melian terracotta relief (detail) showing the return of Ulysses. 460–450 B.C. Height: 7 in. — New York, Metropolitan Museum, Fletcher Fund, 1930, Inv. 30.11.9.

Lit.: Gisela Richter, *Handbook of the Greek Collection* (Cambridge 1953), pp. 79ff., pl. 62a. — Paul Jacobsthal, *Die melischen Reliefs* (Berlin 1931), p. 68, pl. 88. — Franz Müller, *Die antiken Odysseeillustrationen* (Berlin 1913), p. 83, fig. 7.

62 ULYSSES. Bronze statuette from Roman imperial times. Height: 25.5 in.; badly damaged. — Vienna, Kunsthistorisches Museum, Inv. VI–476.

Lit.: Salomon Reinach, *Répertoire de la statuaire grecque et romaine* II (Paris 1897), p. 40, No. 8. — E. Sacken – Sr. Kenner, *Die Sammlungen des Münz- und Antikencabinets* (Vienna 1866), p. 318, No. 1262. — E. Sacken, *Die antiken Bronzen des Münz- und Antikencabinets in Wien* (Vienna 1871), p. 106, pl. 35–36.

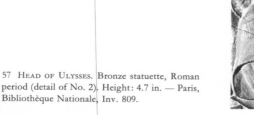

63 THE SUITORS' BANQUET. Alabaster funeral urn. Found in the necropolis of Volterra. Etruscan. Height (without lid): 18.5 in.; width: 30.8 in. — Volterra, Museo Etrusco Guarnacci, Inv. 514.

Lit.: Heinrich Brunn – Gustav Körte, *I rilievi delle urne etrusche* III (Rome 1870), pp. 238ff., 2a. — E. Fiumi, *Studi Etruschi* 25 (1957), p. 395.

64 PENELOPE. Melian terracotta relief (detail) showing the washing of Ulysses' feet. 460–450 B.C. Height: 7.7 in. — New York, The Metropolitan Museum of Art, Fletcher Fund, 1925 Inv. 25.78.26.

Lit.: Gisela Richter, *Handbook of the Greek Collection* (Cambridge 1953), p. 80, pl. 62d. – Paul Jacobsthal, *Die melischen Reliefs* (Berlin 1931), p. 71, pl. 95.

65 THE WASHING OF ULYSSES' FEET. Attic red-figured skyphos by the Penelope-painter, from Chiusi. About 440 B.C. Height: 8 in.; diameter 9.8 in. — Chiusi, Museo Nazionale, Inv. 1831.

Lit. Doro Levi, *Il Museo Civico di Chiusi* (Rom 1935), p. 115, fig. 63a–63b. — J. D. Beazley, *Attic Red-figured Vase-Painters* II (Oxford 1963), p. 1300,2. — Ernst Buschor in Adolf Furtwängler–Karl Reichhold, *Griechische Vasenmalerei* III (Munich 1900ff.), p. 124, pl. 142.

66 ULYSSES RECOGNIZED BY EURYCLEIA. Campana terracotta relief, probably from Tusculum. First quarter of the first cent. A.D. — Rome, Museo delle Terme, Inv. 901.

Lit.: R. Paribeni, *Le Terme di Diocleziano e il Museo Nazionale Romano* (Rome 1932), p. 281, No. 901. — H. von Rohden – H. Winnefeld, *Römische Tonreliefs*, p. 252, pl. 28.

67 ULYSSES AS ARCHER. Attic red-figured skyphos by the Penelope-painter, from Tarquinia. About 450–440 B.C. Height: 7.7 in.; diameter: 9 in. — Berlin, Staatliche Museen (Charlottenburg), Inv. 2588 (2522).

Lit.: Adolf Furtwängler, *Beschreibung der Vasensammlung im Antiquarium* II (Berlin 1885), p. 729, 2588. — Adolf Furtwängler – Karl Reichhold, *Griechische Vasenmalerei* (Munich 1900), p. 138,2. — J. D. Beazley, *Attic Red-figured Vase-Painters* II (Oxford 1963), p. 1300,1.

68 THE SLAYING OF THE SUITORS. Limestone relief from the frieze on the west wall of the Heroon of Gjölbaschi-Trysa (Lycia). First decades of the 4th cent. B.C. Height: *c.* 3 ft. 8 in.; length: 25 ft. — Vienna, Kunsthistorisches Museum.

Lit.: Otto Benndorf, *Das Heroon von Gjölbaschi-Trysa* (Vienna 1889), pl. 7. — Fritz Eichler, *Die Reliefs des Heroons von Gjölbaschi-Trysa* (Vienna 1950).

69 ULYSSES AND PENELOPE. Melian terracotta relief, 460–450 B.C. Height: 7.3 in.; length: 5.7 in. — Paris, Louvre, Inv. 212.

Lit.: Paul Jacobsthal, *Die melischen Reliefs* (Berlin 1931), p. 69, pl. 89.

70 LAERTES' VINEYARD. In the north-west of Ithaca, near Exoge and the Bay of Aphalais. It is in the most fertile part of the island, the area of which is four square miles.

71 ZEUS THE THUNDERER. Bronze statuette from Dodona, by a Peloponnesian master. About 470 B.C. Height: 5.3 in. — Berlin, Staatliche Museen (Charlottenburg), Inv. 10561.

Lit.: A. Greifenhagen, *Antike Kunstwerke* (Berlin 1960), p. 4, pl. 12. — Ernst Langlotz, *Frühgriechische Bildhauerschulen*, p. 69, pl. 37.